Even If Your Heart Would Listen

Even If Your Heart Would Listen

Losing My Daughter to Heroin

ELISE SCHILLER

Published by SparkPress, a BookSparks imprint,
A division of SparkPoint Studio, LLC
Tempe, Arizona, USA, 85281
www.gosparkpress.com

Published 2019
Printed in the United States of America
ISBN: 978-1-68463-008-0 pbk
ISBN: 978-1-68463-009-7 ebk

Library of Congress Control Number: 2019933538

Book design by Stacey Aaronson

Names and identifying characteristics have been changed to protect the privacy of certain individuals.

For Giana

Giana, high school graduation, 1998

Chapter One

Your First Day: January 21, 1980.

Your due date was Super Bowl Sunday. I don't remember who was playing. I do remember sitting on the sofa with Dad, not very interested in the game, waiting. Waiting for you. You know, back then we didn't have ultrasound photos. We didn't have the tests that reveal abnormalities or gender. I wonder now if there was a little nugget inside you, something that would burst into heartache later. I didn't know whom I was waiting for.

I can't remember what the other kids were doing, but I'm sure I was up and down from that sofa numerous times. I remember how enormous I was, and how low I was carrying you. I had gained over forty pounds and wasn't very comfortable. One of Dad's friends stopped by with some cute young girl he was dating. I just remember she was thin, and I was not happy to see her.

At three in the morning, I woke with mild contractions. We timed them and called the hospital, and they said to get in there. But it was the middle of the night, and I didn't want to leave the other kids alone. Around six, we called Dad's parents, and they said they'd come by eight. Then the contractions were stronger, and we decided that we'd better go. So we woke your brother up and told him to hold down the fort until Nannie and Pop-Pop got there. I put out cereal and milk. Dad finally remembered a camera, and the first picture is of me pacing while I'm talking to your siblings on the phone. Not pacing far, because I was speaking from a landline.

I remember absolutely nothing about the labor and delivery except that I was vomiting, as usual, and didn't feel the need for any anesthesia. Dad took pictures, which I have seen, of course, but have not looked at since you died. Can't look at them, don't know if I'll ever be able to look at them.

And then by noon, there you were, completely well and beautiful, with a shock of black hair that stood up like a porcupine's quills. I think Dad was a bit surprised by another girl. I was happy and felt great. An hour or so after you were born, I was taking a shower. You were cozy in a bassinet by my bed, a real sleepyhead. I had to wake you up to nurse.

I wanted to get home. I didn't want to be separated from the other kids. Maybe that was a sign, a bad sign. Maybe I should have been content to have a few days just with you.

~

Your Last Day: January 3, 2014.

It was already January 4 in Philadelphia, not that long after midnight. That Christmas, I had put a cathedral bells ringtone on my phone. It blasted me awake. As soon as I saw a Colorado number I didn't recognize, I was afraid.

It was The Rose House therapist. There must have been a greeting, but I don't recall it. "Giana died tonight." That was what he said.

I replied, loudly I think, "What are you saying?"

"Giana died tonight," he repeated.

I was not fully able to comprehend. Auntie Dina was in the next bedroom, sleeping. I rushed in and shoved the phone at her. "He says Giana's dead, he says Giana's dead." I have no memory of the minutes that she spoke to him, only a vague recollection of her writing things down. I think I was standing in the middle of the bedroom, rocking from side to side.

We had been warned. I knew, at least intellectually, that there was a risk. There had been endless talk and worksheets in rehab about relapse. Your psychiatrist once told you while I was there that the average life of a heroin user is five years from the start of regular use. But I never really thought that you would die, or maybe I couldn't think it. Everything else seemed possible—that you would remain sick, that you would never be able to have a relationship that actually sustained you, that you would lose the career you loved, that you would be sad for the rest of your life. But die? No. Does any parent accept a child's death before the fact, and even then . . . ?

I remember very little about that night or the day after. I called Dad. He was in Florida with his girlfriend and said he was going to start driving right then, in the middle of the night. I called your sister in Colorado who had spent the day with you, that very day. She kept telling me no, it wasn't right, wasn't possible. I said I would get on a plane and go to Colorado, but she said no. I tried to call the other kids, but I don't think I got through right away. I can't remember. My friend James came. I wanted us all to lie down together, with Jade, your dog. Somehow sitting up was impossible. But I kept getting up and going into the bathroom because I was vomiting. I didn't sleep at all.

The next day, your aunts and uncles and a few friends were here. There was a lot of food, but I don't think I ate any. My mouth was dry from the rush of anxiety and adrenaline, and I kept gulping water. Dina answered my phone; people had started to call, but I couldn't talk to them. I don't think I cried a lot, but I might be wrong. Celeste and your brother came, like lost sheep. I remember your sister-in-law lurching into my arms, sobbing, and I was crying immediately, as if she had given me permission to let go. I remember seeing Dad through the high windows of the door. As soon as he saw me, he broke down, saying that he had been determined not to.

I stared at the tennis on the TV, stuck to James's side. My brother gave me medication, and sometime that night I went to sleep.

Giana and her father at the beach, age 2

photo credit: Harvey Finkle

Chapter Two

There are times we remember through a sheen of perfection. Giana's toddler years were such a time. The house was boisterous, noisy, busy, and harmonious. There were seven of us: the four kids; their dad, Lou; myself; and Lou's brother, Uncle D, who lived with us off and on for years. The older kids, Celeste and Greg, were not mine by birth, but they were mine in the heart. They lived with us, even before they started school, and no distinction was ever made, to this day, between my biological and nonbiological kids.

We were all very close to Uncle D. He was the funny, slightly naughty uncle who had lifelong ammunition to make fun of Lou in a way that delighted the kids. Occasionally women turned up in his room, but they never stayed. During that time we had what must have been a VHS of the movie *Mary Poppins*, starring Dick Van Dyke and Julie Andrews, with David Tomlinson and Glynis Johns as Mr. and Mrs. Banks. As toddlers often do, Giana wanted to see the movie again and again, and most of the time she wanted to watch it with Uncle D. Soon the two of them began to march around the house, quoting lines from the movie. The older kids would ask something that they knew would provoke Giana to repeat a line, and then they'd howl with laughter.

"Hey, Giana, is your cereal good? Really good?"

The tiny child would reply with a grin, knowing just what her siblings were waiting for, "It's *supercalifragilisticexpialidocious*!"

Whenever there was a spot of chaos, like a boy tossing clean folded clothes all over the place looking for his baseball shirt, or a bowl of spaghetti inadvertently dumped on the floor, either

Giana or Uncle D would pipe up with "*What's all this? What's all this?*" as Mr. Banks says when he enters the house and finds Mrs. Banks and his children dancing with Dick Van Dyke and a band of chimney sweeps.

Often you don't realize until decades later what the best years of your life have been.

~

Every summer when the children were young, we went to the beach—or, in Philadelphia parlance, we went "down the shore." We went to an island community across a series of causeways. At a certain point crossing the bay, a briny smell erupted, conjuring crisp white wine and the bouillabaisse that I made from time to time at the beach. With two other couples, we owned a dilapidated Victorian house a block from the beach. Each family had a few weeks to themselves, and the rest of the time the house was open for any of us who wished to be there. Our families grew during the time we owned the house. When we were all there together, we numbered about fifteen people, with many friends and relatives passing through during the height of the summer. It certainly had a sixties flavor and was great fun for the children, and usually for the adults. I tend to be a bit of a clean freak, and the inevitable mess was sometimes difficult for me.

My memories of those years range from eight-hour incandescent beach days where the babies slept peacefully under an umbrella to fourteen-hour dreary days trying to entertain children in the rain in a place we had deliberately chosen because it was noncommercial. We read constantly, visiting the little island library at least weekly, and in rainy stretches more frequently. It's hard to imagine now, but we lived there for weeks at a time with no television and no phone. It was, of course, before cell phones and the other electronics we take for granted now. Things improved considerably when my grandmother began renting a house on the bay every summer, all summer, that had a TV, a phone, a dock where we could go crabbing, and occasionally—when my stepfather appeared—a boat! It was a great alternative for the bad-weather days or if someone was sick or if I just needed some adult company.

Giana joined us at the beach for the first time the summer she was six months old. I was teaching then, and not working during the summers. Lou would come down on weekends from the city. This period, the seventies and eighties, rocked from the reverberations of the sixties, except that now we were feeling them as adults with families and careers. Which career got prioritized and who took primary responsibility for the kids was a central question for us and for many of our friends. Our family was not as progressive as some others, partly because of financial reality—a lawyer's salary versus a nursery school teacher's salary—and partly due to family and cultural legacy. Generally I did the childcare, laundry, shopping, cleaning, and errands. The cooking became more shared as time went on. Was this an amicable division of labor? Not always, and as my career prospects grew, it became less so.

It wasn't lost on me that having a gaggle of kids alone at the beach for weeks at a time was not a vacation, especially when it came time to organize that group to get to the beach without another adult present. I remember being atop a dune, Giana in my arms, older kids dragging coolers, sand toys, towels, books, when three-year-old Louisa dropped to her knees and proclaimed, "My feet are too little." Even on the weekends, when Lou showed up, I was primarily in charge. But at least there was someone to send to the fish store, maybe with one or even two of the older kids in tow, someone who might keep an eye on a sleeping baby while I bathed the other kids or took them to the playground, and someone to help drag our endless supplies to the beach. But during the years when Lou was working in California, he was at the beach very little, if at all.

Thank God Giana was such an easy baby. Although she didn't sleep through the night, usually she only woke once and was easy to comfort and get back to sleep. She was a good napper. The rest of the time, she was happy to be carried around or to sit and play. She was small and wiry, not much for me to carry, nor much for *her* to carry, so she was an early crawler and by the end of the first summer was cruising around. The other kids treated her like a toy, which was fine with her. She found these little people who could walk fascinating and funny. I have a picture of her brother, Greg, tossing her in the air while she's wearing a Superman onesie—he called it "playing Superbaby." As a baby she was a pleasure on the beach and didn't do what her older siblings and friends' little ones had done to torture us: she didn't fuss, didn't eat sand, didn't yank off her hat, didn't crawl to other people's blankets and go through their food, didn't cry when the water lapped up over her legs when we sat her down beside us at low tide. As a toddler and preschooler, she loved the beach. She was cautious about the water but not afraid, and she played happily for hours creating sand and water worlds at low tide. When it got too hot, we would sit under the umbrella and sing and read books. When the sky was bright blue, the water refreshing but warm, and the sea breeze gently swaying the flaps of the umbrella, it felt like we were in paradise. But paradise is always an illusion.

People who have spent time at the Jersey shore understand what a very hot and humid summer feels like when you are facing the ocean on one side and the bay on the other. Backdropped by the whine of insects, the day begins with heavy, still air and a morning haze that burns off to a blazing sun. By eleven, the temperature is ninety, matched by the humidity. Everything is damp; the sheets are clammy, the salt sweats, and any box of cereal or bag of pretzels that isn't firmly sealed and refrigerated will be soggy in an hour. There's no remedy but to head for the beach. On happy days, a sea breeze hits you as you cross the dunes, and the temperature drops ten degrees. On unhappy days, the breeze is off the bay and brings with it little black flies that bite, meaning you must stay in the water up to your chin. At some point in the late afternoon, the sun gradually vanishes behind a mackerel sky, the breeze stills, and the humidity seems to rise even higher. The thunderstorm can take hours to build, and by the time it breaks, the air is so heavy with the coming rain that you feel as if you are slogging through molasses. Afterward, instead of relief, the warm air is almost mist.

There is one thing that prospers and propagates in this weather: mold. In an old house like ours, with plaster walls and fraying wallpaper, it bloomed everywhere. And as she grew older, so did Giana's allergy to mold. The closest hospital was on the mainland, a thirty- to forty-five-minute drive depending on the traffic. We had already made a number of trips to the emergency room there: our ungovernable son, who rode his bike without shoes and needed stitches; a child screaming from an ear infection. By the time Giana was six or seven, we were making regular trips there as her asthma spiraled out of control in response to the mold. This was before the days when doctors gave you a nebulizer to take home and the drugs to go in it. We had several different inhalers on top of the oral medication she took, but we learned to tell when the line had been crossed and we had to get into the car and go quickly.

By the time she was eight, going to the beach had become dangerous.

According to her pediatrician, the first sign that Giana might have allergies was the eczema she'd had as an infant. He had prescribed cortisone ointments and cautioned us to be alert. The winter she turned one, we went to visit some friends in Washington. Giana was an early walker and very active, but as the weekend progressed, she became more and more lethargic. Eventually, we realized that she was having trouble breathing. I called the pediatrician, but she began to improve on our drive home. The doctor put it together for us: our friends had a long-haired dog, and likely she was having an asthmatic reaction to the dog hair. We were referred to an allergist, who became a very important figure in Giana's childhood.

Giana's first set of tests, at about age two, revealed allergies to a wide variety of things: virtually all types of animal hair and dander, many plants and trees, and dust. I remember tearing up at the long line of pricks down her little back, and the many that blossomed red and inflamed. In addition, she had recurrent ear infections. Within a week of coming off an antibiotic for an ear infection, she would have another. She was prescribed inhalers, ear tubes, prophylactic antibiotics, and a time release medication that woke her up every night of her childhood at four in the morning and caused frequent vomiting. She got so used to vomiting in the car that she would pipe up quietly, "Pull over," and we all knew what that meant. I got used to my car smelling like bleach. There were countless visits to the allergist and the emergency room, where they gave her the epinephrine that cleared her airways but always caused vomiting. We had to pull up all our rugs, get rid of stuffed animals and house plants, and monitor visits to other people's homes—no cats or dogs. Once a well-meaning volunteer at nursery school handed her a guinea pig to hold; she was covered with hives and gasping for breath within minutes, the EMTs on the way.

The illnesses did not subside, but she learned to cope and rarely complained. On February 2, 1988, just after her eighth birthday, Giana wrote in her journal: "I get sick a lot. But my mom helps me get better. I have ear akcs [*sic*], head akcs, and other stuff. But I always get better!"

Physical activity usually resulted in wheezing. Her doctor recommended swimming, which is often an alternative exercise for asthmatics because the warm moist air in a pool area is easier to breathe during exercise than cool dry air outside. Later her doctor tried taking her off antibiotics, and she began getting ear infections that came on so quickly her eardrums burst and scarred. Back on the antibiotics, she was sent for audiology tests, which showed a slight hearing loss in her worst ear. But she almost never missed school or swim practice. She swam with inhalers next to her water bottle at the end of her lane.

At about age eight or nine, her doctor decided to try allergy shots. Every Monday night for years we went to the doctor's office for the shot, waiting for thirty minutes afterward to make sure there was no reaction. We read and did homework and talked. I have a memory of her lying across several chairs, her head in my lap, as we chatted and waited. I remember a nurse complimenting us, saying we seemed so happy and close that the time spent waiting didn't seem to matter. And it was true. It was our special time alone, away from the other kids and the busyness of our schedules. Years later, those shots paid off when she got a dog and, years after that, went into a veterinary nursing program. She used inhalers all her life and still struggled with eczema, but most of the time she could work around animals without debilitating effects.

When she became ill with anorexia and later with substance use disorder, I wondered about all the attention she had gotten, particularly from me, because of her illnesses. I often talked with her about that, and told her not to act like a victim or cling to being sick because it caused people to give her attention. She recognized the possible connection herself.

In an addiction counseling group note, the counselor wrote:

"Giana then shared one of her goals to work on here [at Caron Treatment Center] being her 'addiction to not being okay,' further describing pain and chaos as ways she feels 'unhealthfully happy.'"

Giana at the beach, age 4

Chapter Three

When Giana was three and a half, we went to Los Angeles for a year so Lou could accept an appointment as a visiting professor. He wanted a change, both of work and location. In addition to his career in criminal defense work, he had been teaching at legal institutes for a long time and was exploring making a change to teaching as his major focus, with trial work as a secondary activity. I had no interest in going to LA and honestly didn't want to go anywhere. I was very happy in our Philadelphia house with our kids and Uncle D. I was working slightly less than full time at a job I really liked—about thirty hours a week and off most of the summer—as the director of a day care center only six blocks from home. I was also getting my master's degree in English, a labor of love but, as I later discovered, a boost to my research and writing skills. We were close to my parents and my in-laws, and I had a supportive network of siblings and friends. Lou traveled a lot, and I relied on that network for childcare and companionship. I had no desire whatsoever to go to a place where I knew almost no one.

Nevertheless, after many quarrels, I reluctantly agreed to go, quitting my job and putting our house up for rent. When I finally made the decision, I did it with the attitude that I would make the best of it and try to be cheerful about it, reminding myself that one can do almost anything for a year. Lou and I went out to LA for a week in the spring, rented a house near the beach, and looked at schools for the kids. I had one class to take to complete my master's coursework, and then exams to pass and a thesis to write. I could do all of it from LA, so that was my plan.

When I was young, I had traveled to India, where I felt more cultural distance than anywhere else I'd ever been. LA came close. Always a winter person, fond of cold and snow, I detested the weather. Arriving in late August, I waited for the autumn that never arrived. What I saw instead was the stripe of yellow smog lining the horizon above the LA bowl. Then a month of rain, followed by six months of drought. It was so dry that my sinuses bled. There was a film of dust on the car every time it wasn't driven for two or three hours. As Christmas approached, I was stunned to discover something called flocking. All these people who had moved to California to escape winter weather had their Christmas tree mounted on a turntable that revolved while a sticky white substance was sprayed on it to resemble snow. Come April, I longed for the stir of spring in the East, the tease of those first mild days with the smell of soggy soil, then the voluptuous growth.

I found our new neighborhood confounding, each house indistinguishable from the one next door. In the beginning, I couldn't even tell which one was ours. Despite their cost and proximity to the beach, many of the houses in our new neighborhood were rentals, filled with other transients looking for utopia. There was no sense of a community with distinguishing characteristics. Most of the houses were beige-and-brown stucco, each with its yard of stones and a confining fence. I was disoriented looking out the window at the landscape of beige on beige and the occasional splash of bougainvillea, not nearly enough to satisfy my desire for the green lawns and lush gardens back East. A big topic of conversation among the neighbors was answering machines, a new thing in LA and unheard of back in Philly.

Giana, do you remember the pool at that house? It was relatively small, surrounded by a tall fence. I was very worried when we rented the house about everybody's safety—keeping neighborhood kids out, keeping you and Louisa safe, keeping your brother from being too wild. I made a rule that no one could go swimming unless I was there, a rule the older kids argued bitterly with me about. Better safe than sorry, I felt. I could imagine your brother coming home with a friend and roughhousing until one of them got hurt, or dunking Celeste until she couldn't breathe, or some such thing. He loved to torment Celeste.

I taught you pre-swimming skills in that pool. You learned the basics of floating, holding on to the side and kicking, blowing bubbles with your face in the water. Louisa already knew a rudimentary freestyle and was comfortable cannonballing into the water. You learned to jump into my arms. You were always more cautious. Sometimes we just floated around on inner tubes and sang and told stories to each other.

Once the year started, it became clear that being a visiting professor takes a lot less time than being a trial lawyer, so Lou had more free time to travel to teaching institutes and to take appellate cases that involved travel to other parts of the country. I felt like he was never there. I recognized without humor the irony that I was the one stuck in LA while he was the one who was elsewhere.

The kids didn't seem to mind at all that he was absent so much. They were used to him traveling a lot—he always had. And when he was gone, the household relaxed. We left lights on and had pancakes for dinner and often all fell asleep in my bed surrounded by books.

It would be reasonable to question why someone renting a

house with a pool near the beach—and who had been relieved of working—would be so miserable. Theoretically I could have gotten a fabulous tan at the beach and the pool while reading as much as I wanted, but that wouldn't work for me. I have always needed to be busy—planning, completing tasks, and accomplishing things, defending myself against my ever-lurking anxiety. So what did I do? Besides taking the class I needed and starting my thesis, I audited enough art history classes to get another master's degree, had I been taking them for credit. I ran miles through the hills near the beach, and I started taking exercise classes at Jane Fonda's studio. Twice a week after school, I put Louisa and Giana in swim lessons and, after their lessons, sat them down with snacks on the pool deck while I swam laps.

On other weekdays after school, we often went to the nearby beach and played in the relentlessly smoggy sunshine. On days off from school, I found myself alone with the kids a lot, driving very long distances to do things we had easily done in Philly with groups of friends, like going to the zoo or a museum. In LA an outing that took two or three hours was bracketed by an hour's drive on each end. When we went to the zoo, we often stayed past rush hour and went to the Griffith Observatory, intriguing for the older kids. I loved the Norton Simon but not so much the drive to Pasadena to get there. The Getty was expanding rapidly, so we went from time to time, even though it wasn't quite the place for the younger kids. Better for them was the Hollywood Walk of Fame and the Natural History Museum. I heard there was a river, and I conjured up grassy banks for picnics, bike paths, and outdoor sculptures. Umm . . . no. The LA River is a flow of water, sometimes just a trickle, through a concrete channel. We went to the LA County Museum of Art, where I was able to dangle the La Brea tar pits as a carrot for the kids. I saw the stink of boiling tar and the fabricated howling of fake mammoths rising from the pit as a perfect metaphor for LA.

Giana didn't seem to care where we went. She was happy

just being with us, going anywhere, except for a lot of car sickness.

My mother and grandmother came out for Thanksgiving, and although it rained most of the time they were there, we went to San Diego for a few days to the famous zoo. We toured the rose garden at USC. I have lovely pictures of them on the beach playing with the kids and reading in our living room to Giana. I had cooked Thanksgiving dinner with my mother and grandmother for my entire life. The relief I felt at having them there made the next six months seem possible.

By the end of the first semester, I had taken the class I needed to complete my coursework, and through an arrangement with the school where Lou was teaching, I took the translation exam that was necessary at that time to get a master's in English—can you translate a piece of literary criticism from a European language to English? I was proceeding with my thesis, on the extremely esoteric topic of the meaning of place in the stage directions of *King Lear*. No, I am not kidding. And it was fifty pages long. In the absence of computers and fax machines, this project was a tedious, complicated, long-distance endeavor. I wrote the thesis drafts in longhand, took them to a typist, and then mailed them to my advisor, who made comments in red pencil and mailed them back to me. The kids wanted to know what I was up to, so I tried to explain and gave a sanitized version of the play to Louisa—more like Cinderella than *King Lear*. No characters getting their eyes put out or killing each other with poison, no old man left outside in a raging storm. Louisa decided she was going to write a child's version of *King Lear* and asked her teacher if it could be their class play—her second-grade class. The woman didn't know the play. It appeared she had never even heard of the play.

Not old enough for school, Giana was enrolled in a church-based preschool close to our rented house. Later, when she came home singing "Onward Christian Soldiers" and pledging allegiance to the Christian flag, I was taken aback, but the space was clean and stocked with appropriate toys and materials, and the people were friendly. In anticipation of the upcoming LA Olympics, the teachers staged their own preschool Olympics, in which Giana happily participated. She did somersault races, walked on a balance beam a few inches off the ground, and pushed other kids in bins that were supposed to be boats. She liked her teachers and her friends. From time to time while I was waiting for comments from my advisor, I would substitute in the elementary classes of the school.

In the late spring, I took the kids to the beach on an unusually warm weekend. Louisa had made a friend, and that little girl and her mother, with baby sister in tow, met us there. We set up our chairs and blanket far enough back that we wouldn't have to move at high tide. After playing for a while with sand toys, Louisa and her friend asked if they could go swimming. Of course Giana wanted to go also. We said yes, and allowed them to walk down to the water's edge. I asked Louisa to hold Giana's hand while I gathered the sand toys and covered up our purses. I told the girls I would be down in a minute and to just wait until I got there. It was very crowded.

No more than three minutes later, I walked down to the water. Louisa and her friend were standing ankle deep in the surf, holding hands, but Giana was nowhere in sight. "Where is your sister?" I gasped. All these years later I can still remember my panic. I sent them back to the blanket and went frantically looking about. I walked toward the jetty, imagining the worst thing possible, that she had gone out into the water alone. Then I took a deep breath and stopped. Did I know my cautious child at all? She would not do that. Reassured that she was simply lost, I walked toward the lifeguard station, which, in addition to an outside chair, had a small enclosure. There she was, big dark eyes peeping out the window. I burst into tears.

As the year progressed, I realized that Lou was doing nothing to indicate that we would be returning to Philly. When I pressed for information about when we were leaving—the day school was over, I hoped—he avoided direct answers. He talked instead about being in LA for the Olympics that summer. Finally, in the early spring, he told me he didn't want to return home yet. He wanted another year to decide what he would do when we went home, perhaps look into teaching jobs in or near Philly. I was wild with anger. I had agreed to one year, and there was nothing about LA that would entice me to stay longer. As soon as school was over, I packed up the kids—except for my son, who stayed with Lou to go to the Olympics—and flew home.

It had been a particularly wet winter and spring back East, and I recall the glorious shock of all that green as I drove from the airport to the home of a friend—of course I couldn't stay in my own house because it was rented. Still, I finally felt as if I could breathe. We went to the beach and spent time with my family. When I left LA, I had not assured Lou that I would be back, but the truth was that we both knew my options were very limited. It was June, I had no job, and I was in the middle of finishing my degree. By early July our house was rented for another year, and all our furniture was in LA, as was my car. Nevertheless, Lou must have thought there was a chance I would stay in Philly anyway because he came East to persuade me to come back to California for just one more year. Just one. And I did agree—for one more year. Unfortunately, this did not feel like an agreement. Right or wrong, it felt as if I was being coerced because I had no viable options and nothing to bargain with. It set up a dynamic of mistrust in a relationship that already had some wide fissures.

Back in LA our previous rental was being sold, so we had to rent a different house and move again. Once more, the packing and unpacking. This house was even closer to the beach but was in the middle of a new development still under construction. There had been no landscaping done, and we were essentially in a dirt pile where construction vehicles started moving around at three in the morning. Yes, I had agreed, but I was trembling with fury much of the time.

In April of that second year, I flew back to Philly during the kids' spring break to take my master's exams. We stayed with my parents and grandmother, and my mother took care of the kids while I spent the day taking the test. My stepfather was recovering from knee replacement surgery, a relatively new procedure at that time, and my mother needed to tend to him, so after the test I spent time helping her by cooking and shopping. I was very worried about him—he was in constant pain and terribly thin. I was disturbed when we had to leave at the end of the week.

Lou waited until I got back to tell me he was not going to return to Philly as he'd promised. He had been offered tenure and was going to take it. He didn't even try to persuade me to stay, knowing that I would not. He didn't say he was never coming home, nor did he say he would. We weren't exactly separating, but we were going to see what happened. I made a few phone calls to friends in Philly and, in a short while, found a job directing a university-based day care center. With most of the furniture in a moving van headed back to Philly, Lou and I decided to drive my car back East, sightseeing with the kids along the way. We were headed into the unknown—a long-distance relationship.

The younger kids seemed to take the changes in stride. The one who had the most difficulty was my son, who was going to stay in LA with Lou. He was a moody teenager and was confrontational with us, especially with Lou, about what was going on. He and I had many difficult phone conversations that year.

The girls seemed to adjust to not being with their older brother, especially since they were reminded continually that he would be back in Philly for Christmas and that we would go to California and Disneyland for spring break. After we had been back for a while, Giana wrote in her journal: "Sometimes it is hard to have an older brother. But usuley [*sic*] they are okay. But I usuley don't get to see my brother because he lives in California. But I get to talk to him a lot too." Yes, there were daily phone calls. We had very large long-distance bills.

Once I decided to move back to Philly, I had to find schools —again. Giana was five, turning six in January. At that time Philadelphia had an unusually late kindergarten cutoff, allowing children who would be five by January 31 to enter. But in Los Angeles, Giana had missed the cutoff and had thus spent two years in preschool. I went to the neighborhood school to enroll her and was shocked when I was told that she would be placed in first grade. "But she hasn't gone to kindergarten," I kept repeating.

"Her birthday is her birthday," they replied, "and it's first grade for her." I took my argument to the principal, then to the regional superintendent, and finally to the superintendent's office. I felt as if I was in some Kafkaesque elementary school drama, or perhaps a parody of a Kafkaesque elementary school drama. A very sympathetic man in the superintendent's office told me that there was nothing they could do; it was matter of state funding, district funding, complicated rules (probably beyond a mother's understanding). "Really? What about the needs of the child," I pressed.

"Sorry, ma'am."

So that is how Giana and Louisa ended up in a private K–12 Quaker school, where they received an exceptional academic and values-based education, and our neighborhood elementary school lost an involved and knowledgeable parent. I could have put Louisa in public school, but I'd already done the kids in different schools, the multiple home and school association meetings, the various fundraisers, the conflicting back-to-school nights . . . and the different commutes. Not again.

In the end, this school was the place where Giana was the

most comfortable in her life, attending for thirteen years. In her yearbook a close friend wrote: "Giana, Giana, Giana, I know you know this, but you seem a little depressed about school ending. Be happy, sweetie! You've worked your whole life to be here!" But I don't think she was ever that happy again.

Although Lou returned to Philly several years later and we lived together for some time, our relationship never recovered.

~

In addition to the beach, our other regular destinations were Colorado and Rome, both tied to Lou's work. When the kids were young, we went to Colorado numerous summers for a month. Generally we rented a rustic cabin at the Chautauqua in Boulder, one of the last remaining sites of the old Chautauqua circuit, which still retained the original mission of providing cultural offerings, including a speaker series, concerts, and plays in a large auditorium on the site. Nestled up against the Flatiron foothills, there were meadows and hiking trails right out our back door, as well as a playground and tennis courts on the grounds. Lou worked, and I spent busy days with the kids in outdoor activities, including swim lessons at one of Boulder's great recreational facilities and, as they got older, sports and day camps. On weekends, we would drive up to Rocky Mountain National Park and hike, ride horses, and picnic. It was idyllic, and it was no surprise when years later Louisa decided to do her graduate school internship in Boulder and eventually settled nearby.

As everybody got older, Giana was occasionally the only child we had with us if we traveled. One summer, Lou was teaching a seminar in Colorado, and we went, taking my mother and Giana, who must have been fifteen or sixteen. Lou may have been there longer, but the rest of us stayed for about two weeks. I remember a weekend trip to the hot springs and an outdoor performance of the University of Colorado's Shakespeare Festival where the fickle Colorado weather made for a freezing evening as we watched the rarely produced *Titus Andronicus*. I don't remember a lot more about that trip except that Giana spent a lot of time weeping. She had left behind a boyfriend—I've no memory of which one—and she was miserable. I was impatient with her about it, having gone through similar boyfriend drama with Louisa and Celeste. I remember telling her she was overreacting, to enjoy herself and we would be home soon, and other similar platitudes. I have wondered since whether I should have taken her heartache more seriously.

There were so many things like that, which would have been forgotten or seemed insignificant were it not for what happened later.

Swim Team photo, age 12

Chapter Four

"When I was a child, I loved to *swim*." That was how Giana filled in the blank on one of the many rehab worksheets, this one an exercise to "find the inner child."

Giana had exercise-induced asthma, among other health issues, making it difficult for her to play games that involved running. Her doctor had recommended swimming. That was convenient because Louisa was swimming on a YMCA team, so Giana began taking swim lessons at the same facility, with ear plugs and a tight cap. After a few months, the coach approached me and said it seemed silly for me to be coming and going so frequently with practices for one kid and lessons for the other. He'd make it easy for me and put Giana in the practice lane with his newest and slowest kids, and she would learn to swim that way. She was five or six. Six months later she was competing.

Giana was an inveterate journal writer all her life. From her journal (the spelling is hers): September 23, 1988 (age eight):

I am on two swim teams, a winter one and a summer one. My winter one is at the Roxboroh YMCA. I like it there. It's been fun but are coch is hard. I've been on my winter swim team for 3 years. My sister is also on it. My summer one is flour town swim club.

Are practisies are hard. We have to do a lot of work. We have to swim a lot of laps. Warm ups is usualy a 200. Then we usualy do 50s. At the end of each parctisie we usualy parctise are flip turns. Then it's time to go.

She was a skinny little girl with a lion's heart. She loved to compete, and she loved to win. I remember the first time she had to dive into the pool rather than start in the water. She froze. Her coach ran over and gently pushed her into the water, and like a wind-up toy, she started churning toward the other end. She won.

The Y team practiced and competed only during the school year, so Giana also joined the team at our swim club. It was primarily a fun summer activity, with many kids who didn't swim in the winter and thus weren't very fast. Whatever the level or the seriousness, Giana most definitely loved to swim. Those summer practices were funny to watch, with kids at all different levels swimming over and around each other. Giana was double-jointed in both her elbows and knees. When she stood, her knees bowed out behind her. When she leaned on her hands against the floor or a table, the inside of her arms bowed outward quite significantly. It was a bit disconcerting, but the extra flexibility was an asset in the water. Even in a crowded pool, I could spot her immediately because her arms rose out of the water at such odd angles.

When Giana was ten, her coach at the Y told us that there was nothing more he could do for her and we should move her to a more competitive team. He gave us a recommendation, and along with several other swimmers, she made the transition. She was placed in a developmental group with an assistant coach. The new club was very different, starting with the water temperature. The Y pool had been heated to appeal to all age groups, including very young children getting swim lessons and older people doing water exercise. The new pool was cold by comparison, and the work load was much greater. Giana's group practiced six times a week. But after a tough first week and a few tears, she adjusted, and soon she couldn't wait to get there every day. This was a year-round USA Swimming team with a robust meet schedule. Giana thrived on the competition. She made rapid progress, and in addition to the shorter distances in freestyle and backstroke that she had swum at the Y, she began to swim the 200-yard freestyle and the individual medley.

The transition to this team was a transition for me as well. In addition to the extra driving due to the daily practice schedule, there was a greater expectation of parent participation. This was a public recreation team, with low fees but lots of fundraising and parent tasks. The parents did the computer work for the meets, kept track of fees, bought the equipment, made arrangements for the team's travel, and volunteered at meets. There were kids whose parents were conspicuously absent, but it was the culture of the team that other parents picked up the slack and supported all the kids who wanted to swim.

The team was majority black, and the coaches were black, although, not surprisingly, as its success grew, more white swimmers joined. We lived in an integrated neighborhood, I worked in a majority black setting, and the older kids went to public schools that were diverse. Still, this was a different experience because serious swimming is such an all-encompassing activity. Giana spent the majority of her time outside of school with kids who were not white. Both she and I got an education when we traveled to meets and were met with frosty politeness by the parents and coaches of the ubiquitous white teams, when our coach lectured the kids about needing to behave better than anyone else because we would be judged like nobody else, and when Giana, naked in the shower, heard racist comments about her teammates made by other white kids showering next to her. But without skirting any issues, the coaches on our team fostered a strong camaraderie among the swimmers and their parents. It was a unique environment.

The kids Giana's age swam meets at all levels of competition. Some meets did not require that the swimmer meet a qualifying time, while others did. Some were dual meets against one other team, completed in a few hours; others were large two- or three-day meets with dozens of teams participating. Everyone loved the Princeton meet, held every fall in December at the university. This was a regional three-day meet held close to Christmas when the pool was available for rental, and it required meeting certain qualifying times. The team stayed together in a small hotel that we booked as early as September. The swimmers tried hard throughout the fall to make the entry times for their various age groups and events. The meet format was grueling if a swimmer had a number of individual events and relays: as many as three events each morning and, if lucky enough to make the finals, those same events at night. Giana had been swimming with her new team less than a year when she qualified to go to the Princeton meet in a wide range of events.

She had never swum the 500-yard freestyle (twenty 25-yard laps) in competition and was seeded in the middle with a time that the coach must have made up. In her heat, she was a low seed and thus placed in an outer lane. As usual, the coach positioned himself on the deck near her lane, several stopwatches in hand. By the eighth lap, it was clear that she was swimming fast, in a position to win the heat. The coach started walking up and down on the deck beside her lane, yelling louder with each lap. Teammates on deck began to yell, hoping she could hear them each time she turned her head to breathe. In the stands, parents began hollering and ringing cowbells. She finished with an excellent time and placed in the top eight.

That evening in the hotel restaurant where all the swimmers and parents gathered to eat after finals, the head coach came by to congratulate her. "Shouldn't I be moving up to your group?" she asked. He hedged and she persisted. "All my times dropped. A lot." He finally relented, and so things changed again. Six practices a week turned into eleven, as this faster group practiced every morning before school as well as after. She was the youngest swimmer in the group and quickly became the little sister, the mascot of the older girls. They were very kind and supportive of her, even when she eventually was faster than some of them. Giana began to "swim up"—that is, she no longer swam in her age group but in the "open division," where anyone could swim if they could meet the qualifying times. The following summer, when she still wanted to go to overnight camp for two weeks, the coach balked. No way could she miss two weeks of practice and still go to the championships at the end of the summer. She convinced him that she would practice daily at camp, so he reluctantly wrote workouts on index cards, and we covered them with clear contact paper so they wouldn't get ruined when they got splashed while she was swimming. The camp agreed to let her have a lane in the pool for ninety minutes when lessons were scheduled, and she practiced.

That summer all her times dropped, and on the final day of summer championships, she won several events. She was so happy and proud of herself. That was a great day.

And there were more great swimming days, but there were lots of very difficult ones. As she got older, her progress slowed. This is common as girls develop, and many never swim faster than they did at age fifteen or sixteen. This wasn't true for her, but the improvement in her times became incrementally smaller. Her response was to work harder. And harder. She was regarded by her teammates and coaches as one of the hardest workers and was often recognized for this, but that was not the recognition that she wanted. She wanted to win, always. Over time, failing to meet her own goals whittled away at her confidence and self-esteem. During this period, she saw a therapist for a while, someone who had a history of working with athletes.

There were several times when she decided to quit. Sometimes I let her, but she always came back. She had become a good athlete in other sports as well, especially field hockey, which she played at school.

What if I had been more neutral, blown off her coach when, after tenth grade, he told her she had to choose, that she couldn't continue to miss swim practices to attend field hockey practices?

The college application process was very different for Giana than it had been for her siblings. It was all about swimming. Which schools wanted her, which schools were offering money, which teams her coach wanted, which teams she wanted. Giana was insistent on choosing a school where there was room for her to grow as a swimmer. Now I look back and think what a mistake we made.

What if we had pushed her to choose a school where she would have been one of the fastest swimmers—there were plenty of those recruiting her. Would that have been the confidence boost she needed?

She swam at school as well as on her club team and, almost twenty years since her graduation, still holds a record at her high school. But the big goals she had for herself never materialized. All of this is very relative, but she was measuring herself against the most successful swimmers on her team, a few of whom went to Olympic Trials, and the best club swimmers her age in the country. She was rarely happy with her results. This was a theme in other areas of her life. She was never happy with her physical appearance. She made honors with every report card and was equally good in all subjects, but she compared herself negatively to the kids who took several AP classes a year instead of one, or the one or two who came close to perfect SAT scores.

Sitting on a bookshelf in my study is the Most Valuable award she received from her school swim team the year she graduated, along with a picture of her signing her Division I college contract.

Giana signing her Division I contract with her parents and the school athletic director

Chapter Five

For a long while, I had a reproduction of a Picasso drawing hanging in my house. It is called *Mother and Child and Studies of Hands,* dated 1904. A young woman is nursing her baby, its plump arm stretching up with its little hand cupping her face. The mother's dark hair is mostly swept up, but a few long pieces tumble down. She has large sober eyes, a long nose, and a thin but shapely mouth. She always reminded me of Giana. The mother is looking down at her child with a troubled expression. For one who has so recently given birth, she appears very thin. Most noticeably, her shoulders are misaligned, almost grotesquely so. One would be slightly higher than the other, holding the baby as she is, but not to this extreme. In contrast, her hands are beautiful, delicate, with slim fingers posed elegantly, much as Giana's were. There are quickly drawn studies of hands below the figure group and to the side.

In the fall of 1999, I was packing stuff to take Giana to her second inpatient stay for anorexia. When I looked up, she was sitting on the bed, legs tucked under swiveled hips, head at an odd angle, shoulders misaligned. Her large dark eyes were staring at nothing. She was almost unresponsive, catatonic. Her hands were holding her forearms, the skin on her long elegant fingers translucent.

I have never been able to look at that drawing since.

In the spring of Giana's first year of college, 1999, I went to her swim team banquet, which was held a few weeks after championships but before studying for final exams began in earnest. It had been a disappointing year. She'd expected to improve her race times in at least a couple of events, but when the Big Ten league championships rolled around, the times of her important events were slightly slower than her best times. She wasn't the only one, but it was a blow. With the incredible facilities and the changes in training, she had expected gains. She was grim and quiet.

At the banquet a few weeks later, Giana looked spectacular, wearing a short skirt and skimpy top that highlighted every lean muscle. Along with many of the other girls on the team, she had gotten a small dolphin tattoo on the upper part of her back. She seemed to have accepted her less than stellar performance at champs and was moving on. The coach complimented Giana and a few other girls who had volunteered to do an extra weights routine in addition to the usual maintenance workouts in the pool. That didn't surprise me; hard work was her forte. The banquet was a sit-down dinner with a choice of entrées. When they brought the entrées out, Giana turned hers away and asked for something else. I thought that was odd, because, except for fish and mushrooms, she ate everything. But this day was for communing and celebrating, and I didn't think about it again.

A month or so later, at the beginning of May, I went up to Rutgers to help Giana bring home all her stuff for the summer. As soon as I saw her, I was alarmed. She had her hair in braids, and her face looked extremely thin. Always lean, she had never been able to get her weight above 142, which was a little under what her longtime club coach would have liked but acceptable for a 5'9" athlete. I raised the question right away—what's going on; how much weight have you lost? She blew me off and told me that she had been working out very hard. I kept asking questions over the next week as I saw her choosing only a very narrow group of foods, all of them low in calories. She started swimming again with her club coach, as many college swimmers do in the summer. He was very unhappy about her weight loss, about twelve pounds, blaming it on the "idiot college coaches" who often emphasized low weight for females and did weigh-ins on a regular basis.

Finally, after about ten days, Giana called me at work and told me she wanted to talk. We agreed to meet along the river, and demonstrating that I really didn't understand what was happening, I stopped and got us tuna hoagies. She pushed the hoagie aside and told me that I had been right; she was restricting food. She told me that she was preoccupied all the time with what she was eating, that she couldn't stop thinking about it. I sprang into action and made an appointment with her doctor, a pediatrician. She hadn't yet switched to a family doctor for adults as she more frequently visited her allergist and had seen a gynecologist. To my amazement, the doctor didn't think there was a serious problem. That was the last time Giana ever saw her. We got her to a therapist who specialized in eating disorders, and she got Giana to a different doctor. Generally Giana went to the therapist on her own—she was nineteen—but at times Lou or I went with her. Giana's grasp on reality fluctuated. Sometimes she understood that her behavior was self-destructive and had to change, while at other times she struggled to acknowledge the problem and lapsed into silence when confronted with the possible consequences. Attempts to get her to talk about her feelings and thoughts were mostly unsuccessful.

Meanwhile, the range of foods she ate and the size of the portions declined, and she grew thinner and thinner. By sometime in late June, Giana's coach told her that she couldn't continue to swim if she kept losing weight. I reminded her that her Division I scholarship depended upon summer swimming; it was part of the agreement. It didn't help. As soon as the coach barred her from practice, she started running. I remember watching her sprint across the lawn and around the corner the very day she could no longer swim. I had no idea what to do. I was still at the point of trying to reason with her and persuade her to eat, offering her a zillion different possible foods: how about frozen yogurt with fruit and nuts, how about protein shakes, how about ratatouille? We were in a situation that eventually became familiar, trying to keep an eye on Giana while regular life proceeded—I was working, her older siblings were in school or working or both, her father was working. The plan for her summer was to swim twice a day. Without that plan in place, she was alone, all of her friends swimming, and she was starving herself.

I have a distinct memory of the Fourth of July that year. I was sitting on the front porch of our family house, where I no longer lived since my separation from Lou two years earlier. On this evening he was out of town. I was crying. I had offered to take Giana to see the fireworks, not something we typically did, but anything to escape the suffocation of the eating disorder. When she refused, I went outside. She was sitting inside in the den, which abutted the porch. Through the open window I could hear that she was watching the Food Channel. The Food Channel! Who could understand this? I felt as if I was going crazy, and I was certain she was. The thing is, almost everyone else did not think so. They thought it was a stubborn, manipulative way of getting attention, as she so often had with her various illnesses, a way of avoiding the hard work of summer swimming without having to say *no*, a way of driving her father and me crazy because of our separation. "For God's sake, just eat" was the general response.

Later, in her journal, Giana mused about this as well. "I think this might be all about attention. I was always the skinny one who ate so much. I'm used to being 'the skinny one.'"

Shortly afterward, her therapist told us that Giana was not getting well and that she needed inpatient treatment. I was completely onboard with that, feeling frightened and confused about how best to help. Fortunately, the therapist was well connected to the Renfrew Center, and fortunately, this facility was close to us in Philadelphia. Giana would be there as a resident three times over the next year. It was our first experience with inpatient rehab. Like the other private rehab institutes we would get to know, Renfrew is located in a bucolic setting on the edge of the city. Set in a small valley surrounded by woods, a fountain tinkling in a landscaped courtyard, Renfrew feels serene, despite the struggles of its residents. There was one difference between the experience at Renfrew and the treatment centers that were yet to come: at Renfrew Giana was generally treated by highly qualified medical and clinical professionals. Her primary caregivers were nurses, dieticians, masters-level therapists, and doctors.

Initially, the emphasis was on stabilizing her physical health, which included restrictions on her mobility until she gained weight. She was surprised and sullen when Renfrew staff wouldn't even let her walk for exercise until she had gained a certain amount of weight. After she was given permission, she and I walked up and down the Renfrew driveway. The number of times an anorexic patient was permitted to make this circuit depended on how much weight she was gaining. Giana was assigned a dietician who began working with her to restore a diet of adequate calories and nutritional content. I remember her stubborn refusal to follow the recommendations and the great anxiety that mealtimes created. She wrote continually in her journal about undermining her treatment: "I went down this morning and they gave me a supplement and I poured it down the toilet." At a certain point she was supposed to be eating 4,300 calories a day, but she managed to reduce that by not using cream in her coffee and skimping on spreads like mayonnaise and butter, or by cutting off all the fatty parts of meat and stealthily depositing them in her pocket or her bra.

In addition to medical treatment she was assigned a therapist and participated in individual and group sessions. There was a weekly family session that we were "required" to attend, led by one of the therapists. The facilitator always reminded us to be respectful of the patients, anorexics and bulimics, all female, as they spoke. Many seemed in great despair, while others spoke of things that were very superficial, like a young wife's anger at a husband who didn't want her to get a belly button ring. But given the extremity of eating disorders, I felt that these seemingly trivial reflections were simply a cover-up for something else. Typical for Giana, she never spoke in this larger group.

Keeping her in residential status entailed a constant negotiation between the insurance company and the Renfrew staff. The insurance company wanted to step her down to a less intensive level after she'd gained three pounds. Literally. Eventually she was discharged to partial hospitalization status, and we paid the difference between that and residential treatment in order to keep her there around the clock. I reminded myself frequently that we were incredibly lucky to have good insurance and good jobs. I knew there were people out there struggling with eating disorders and mental health issues who were not getting treatment.

When Giana began restricting her eating, she started smoking. Smoking! A person with severe asthma! An athlete! I noticed at Renfrew that almost everyone smoked. Studies do show that nicotine suppresses appetite, so it seems Giana intentionally began smoking as she restricted her food intake. I also speculate that the repetitive behavior of smoking soothed her.

Later, when she moved to Vermont and started swimming again, she stopped. In the years after, she was running, working out in the gym, and doing yoga. But at some point—I don't know exactly when, but I know it was linked to the worsening of her mental illness and to her substance use disorder—she began smoking again. By the time she entered drug rehab for the first time, she was smoking, and so, it seemed to me, was everybody else in rehab. It was ubiquitous in every facility Giana attended.

There are estimates that upward of 70 percent of people with substance use disorder smoke, compared to just above 15 percent of the American adult population. The National Institute on Drug Abuse (NIDA), part of the National Institutes of Health, reports that tobacco use is also particularly high among people with anxiety and depression.

Giana was afflicted with all three—substance use disorder, anxiety, and depression—so her tobacco use is not at all surprising. People who are already wired for addiction through heredity, environmental factors, stress, and mental health disorders are at a much higher risk. Tobacco addiction works in much the same way as other substance use disorders. According to NIDA, "nicotine increases levels of the neurotransmitter dopamine in these reward circuits, which reinforces the behavior of taking the drug." In this case, the drug is the addictive property in tobacco—nicotine—which is a central nervous system stimulant.

I couldn't understand and still don't understand why smoking was not addressed at Renfrew or at any of the drug rehabs.

After three weeks, Giana left residential treatment and stepped down to the intensive outpatient program, which included three group sessions a week at Renfrew, and she returned to her private therapist. If she was anxious, I was more so. I was constantly asking her what she had eaten that day, adding up calories in my head. I tried tricks like slipping Ensure into smoothies and flouring chicken breasts, using butter instead of olive oil to sauté them. It wasn't too effective because she cross-examined me and anyone who was cooking about exactly how the food was being prepared and what ingredients were used. Restaurants were impossible.

It was August and time to think about school. Her treatment professionals were against her returning to school, but she was adamant about it and convinced her father that it was the right course. I was ambivalent; part of me thought she'd be motivated by being back on campus and among friends. But she was still a fragile weight, below 120, and my intuition told me that without supervision, she might not be able to be compliant. The characterization of addiction also applies to compulsive coping behaviors, like anorexia: *unable to change the behavior even when you are aware of and experiencing the negative consequences.*

Giana had started at Rutgers still seeing her (last) high school boyfriend, but that had fizzled quickly as college life and the new team took over. During freshman year, she lived in an athletic dorm with a swim team roommate. She used to describe walking from the dorm to practice at five in the morning while nonathletes were stumbling back to their dorms after a night of partying. The swimmers made few friends outside the team—how would there be time? Giana described some parties at a house that some of the older swim team guys rented, but I don't recall being too worried about that. She was taking a full academic load, practicing twice a day, and working out in the gym with the football strength coach. Parties? Really? At some point during the year, she became attached to a kid on the swim team. I met him a few times, saw him swim: an average-looking kid who I think was a backstroker. There were some contacts with him during her time at Renfrew, and before school started, she went to visit him at his parents' home. I don't know exactly what happened, but I think that he began pulling away from her even while she was still at Renfrew. Her visit sealed the deal. I wouldn't be surprised if his parents reacted very negatively to their relationship—he was on a swimming scholarship, and here he was involved with a girl who obviously had major problems and wasn't going to be able to swim. The fracture in this relationship exacerbated the emotional issues that were already there, her sadness and her anxiety, but she still insisted on going back to school.

When Giana returned to school, she was still not well enough to swim, but due to arrangements already made, she moved into a house with other swimmers. It was agreed that she would "weigh in" with the campus health service twice a week, and she signed a release that they could contact us if she didn't at least maintain her current weight. Nothing went well. Her roommates and friends were all swimming, and although some were sympathetic, anorexia is such an extreme behavior that it can be frightening and confusing for others to witness. Feeling this, mingled with shame, anorexics often isolate, and Giana did just that. She was also breathless with anxiety over her ex-boyfriend, who was swimming and socializing normally. She only lasted a few weeks before I got the dreaded phone call from the campus doctor. I could tell that she was in a downward spiral anyway, just by talking with her on the phone. I drove up to school, got a hotel room, and convinced her to come and stay the night with me. I recall sitting in the hotel restaurant, where she ordered a bowl of fruit. She was keeping track of every calorie she ate, limiting herself to four hundred a day. She told me with complete conviction that she could live with her anorexia and manage the rest of her life. She was delusional.

So only six weeks after going back to school, she came home again and reentered Renfrew, this time at just under a hundred pounds. After a psychiatric assessment, she was started on a cocktail of drugs to deal with depression, anxiety, and severely distorted body image. There was discussion of obsessive-compulsive disorder, and Giana revealed that as a child she had often secretly performed two behaviors commonly associated with OCD, ritual counting and lock checking. I was bewildered when it was explained to us that she actually saw her body not as emaciated but as large and full, Rubenesque—distorted vision, distorted thinking, a form of psychosis. I believe there were five drugs in all. This is when Giana received her first official diagnosis of major depressive disorder and generalized anxiety disorder, as well as anorexia. Renfrew put her on bed rest, meaning she could not get up except to use the bathroom.

I left my job and visited her every day. I recall being outside with her sitting at the fountain one day after she had gained enough weight to be out of bed. She was not talking, not responding to questions I was asking. I was exasperated and finally asked, "Don't you want to get well?"

And she replied, "I don't know." The hair on my neck bristled, and I felt my skin turn to gooseflesh. Another day when I was pressuring her to talk, she turned to me and said, "Maybe you should leave." She and I had a few tough therapy sessions during this time, when she opened up about how sad she was about her father's and my separation, our other relationships, and her feelings of anger, especially toward me.

That fall, not working, I spent quite a bit of time at my parents' home. The visiting hours at Renfrew were thirty minutes during the week in the late afternoon, with lengthier times on weekends. My mother and my stepfather—who was my father and my children's grandfather in every way but biology—lived in a large apartment in the suburbs. My mother had remarried shortly after my father died, when I was a teenager. For many years, my grandmother had lived in an adjoining apartment. When my grandmother moved in, my parents had broken through a wall separating the adjacent outside decks, as well as the wall separating the two laundry rooms. Thus one could pass easily from one apartment to the other, either through French doors and across the now large deck or through the pantry and laundry room area. Both apartments had two bedrooms and two full baths, as well as spacious L-shaped living and dining rooms. And two kitchens, making this the perfect place for large family gatherings—*four* bathrooms!—and a very convenient crashing point for various children, eventually with their children in tow. My children had spent many nights in this quirky space and had attended many family gatherings entertained by the toys, games, and books for various-aged children tucked away in drawers and baskets. This arrangement served my parents and grandmother well for about eighteen years, until my grandmother died in the summer of 1999, a few weeks short of her 103rd birthday.

My mother was unable to address cleaning out my grandmother's apartment. She did not move to empty the apartment or tell the landlord it was no longer needed, even under pressure from my siblings and me. While it was convenient for my children and nomadic nieces and nephews, and there were frequent guests, it was an unjustifiable expense. It would be almost five years before my mother was able to let it go. It contained many pieces of furniture, china, silver, jewelry, paintings, books, and family documents that had been passed down through multiple generations. My grandmother had been the oldest and the only girl of four children; not surprisingly, she became the keeper of most of it. So on those mornings that I visited my parents, I also packed up clothes, preserved letters and photographs and documents, and sorted everyday dishes and cutlery from china and silver that needed to be saved.

My mother was a very warm and affectionate person who had the gift, as my sister so eloquently described years later at her memorial service, of making you feel like being with you, talking to you, was the one and only thing that she had any desire to do. However, she was not a master of organization. Thus, my grandmother and I had spent time when she was in her nineties going through some of her documents, labeling photographs, and talking about her life, often while Giana read or did homework nearby. I recorded some of those conversations. She was my only grandparent—the others had died or disappeared long before I was born—and I was very close to her.

For her part, during the five years that my grandmother's apartment remained, my mother kept her many African violets alive.

Giana was hospitalized until Thanksgiving. When she left Renfrew, she was still thin but at a safe weight. I believe she was discharged two days before the holiday, and while she did not participate at all in the food preparation, she did clean, arrange flowers, and set out candles. But this is what she wrote about it:

I realize that I hate big things. Like Thanksgiving. I hate how there is so much food and preparation and time. It stresses me out that my mom has to go to so many different stores and cook at two different houses [she means with my mother] and everything is so messy. But why? What does that affect me so much? This disease is the easiest way to simplify your life and that's what I've always wanted—my life to be very simple and tidy and clean. And I have to be productive. I have to be doing something . . . Like today my mom and I went for errands and I felt unproductive because I didn't get out of the car at one store.

Giana's penchant for productivity, organization, and planning was something she shared with me and her sisters. In the old days, there were planners, address books, journals—sometimes several journals going at once, one for work and one personal—and sticky notes. The joy of checking off the to-do lists! Celeste and I have moved a lot of that to an electronic format, but Louisa still maintains it all in hard copy. For all of us, it's an attempt to control.

Still, after this inpatient stay, Giana seemed more communicative, more positive, and more realistic about her next steps. She realized she would not be going back to school on a swimming scholarship. As we moved from Thanksgiving to Christmas to full-blown winter, Giana started to gain more weight. She was still on medication, doing an outpatient program at Renfrew, and seeing a therapist. In January, her academic plans uncertain, she enrolled in a class at Temple University, where Lou was now a law professor. We figured the credits would transfer, whatever she decided to do. She enjoyed being back in school and breezed through the class. My recollection is that she was doing no serious exercise.

I took a new job.

That winter we were beginning to plan for Celeste's wedding, to take place in August. Giana and Louisa were bridesmaids. We all agreed that we wanted to pick dresses that could be worn again, so we went with Nicole Miller cocktail dresses. In high school, Giana's prom dresses had been size 8 or 10, depending on the cut. They sometimes had to be altered at the waist, but her back and shoulders were so broad from swimming that anything smaller wouldn't fit. When we originally ordered the bridesmaid dresses, Giana was still in the grip of her anorexia. She told me to order her a size 2, which at that time would have been large for her, but she was making a concession to the idea that she would eventually be gaining weight. We talked and argued and negotiated back and forth, and in the end we agreed that I would order a size 6. Louisa, shorter but curvier, would also get a size 6.

In late spring of that year, 2000, a few months before the wedding, my sisters and I decided we wanted to take our parents on a memorable vacation. They were getting older, and we were concerned about my stepfather's health. We wanted a vacation with them before it was no longer possible (and we were prescient; my stepfather never traveled again). One of my sisters was living in Malaysia due to her husband's employment, so we decided to meet in Hawaii. Three sisters, two parents, and a gang of kids ranging from seven to twenty-three. My sister the bargain hunter planned the trip and found beautiful and relatively inexpensive accommodations on the garden island of Kauai. Our parents got a bedroom to themselves, of course; I was sharing a room with Giana, Louisa, and one niece. That bit of crowding didn't matter, because who cared about being indoors? Except for my stepfather, we all swam, the kids surfed, we hiked in the amazing Kauai gorges, and we rode horses on the beach. He sat on the balcony and looked at the sea, and went with us on a whale watching/snorkeling excursion (no snorkeling for him). Giana joined the kids roughhousing in the water. It was heavenly.

Giana had gained all her weight back and then some. I think this was the heaviest she had ever been. While most people would not have considered her overweight, she was clearly uncomfortable with the change in her body—the weight, of course, but also the lack of muscle tone compared to her swimming body. One night my mother, my sisters, my daughters, and I had a girls' night out, leaving my father and the younger kids at the hotel. After cocktails and a delicious dinner, I was in a bathroom stall when I heard vomiting in the stall next to me. I looked down and there were Giana's shoes. Giana had gone from starving herself to binging and purging. I confronted her about it that night after we left the restaurant, and she acknowledged the behavior. We discussed treatment plans.

Back from Hawaii, Giana reentered Renfrew for two weeks of treatment for the bulimia. Perhaps the past year of treatment had kicked in, because there was a quick positive change in her attitude and demeanor during this hospitalization. When she was discharged, although still on medication and in outpatient treatment, she seemed much more like the Giana of earlier years. While she had gained a handle on the binging and purging, she was heavier than she wanted to be, almost 150 pounds. The challenge was to get to a healthy weight that she could accept, somewhere between 135 and 140 pounds. Her therapeutic "support team" advised her to move toward that very slowly and helped design a healthy nutrition and exercise plan.

Meanwhile, wedding planning lurched into high gear. And as it did, it became clear that Giana's size 6 was not going to work at all. I was unable to return her dress by this point, and there was no way it could even be altered to fit. I ordered another dress, size 14. Louisa, meanwhile, was working and enrolled in graduate school. Always very athletic, she was becoming a serious runner, and her body was changing. In her size 6, she looked as if she was wearing a whale costume. The day before the wedding, I had her standing on a table, straight pins between my lips, and with my limited sewing skills, I was altering the dress.

So after the lovely wedding we had a size 14 dress; a size 6 dress, never worn; and a size 6 dress that had been poorly altered to about a 4. None of those dresses were ever worn again.

Chapter Six

During the Christmas–New Year holiday, 2000–2001, Lou took the daughters to Vermont on a ski trip. I talked to them once or twice while they were there; everybody seemed to be having fun. Giana had taken classes in the fall at Temple, and her weight had stabilized at a healthy number. She had been weaned off some of the medication and was now just taking two drugs, down from five. We were beginning to talk about what was going to happen next. Go back to Rutgers? Officially transfer to Temple? We assumed the decision would be made with the following school year in mind.

After the ski trip, Celeste and her husband headed to nearby Montreal to vacation. Lou made the mistake of starting for home with the forecast of a winter storm looming and eventually had to stop and check in to a motel. Louisa called me to let me know that they would not be home when expected. I asked to talk to Giana and was told she wasn't with them. Wasn't with them? Where was she? Lou got on the phone and told me that while in Vermont, Giana had taken a snowboarding lesson, become infatuated with the instructor, and decided to stay in Vermont with him. I was not happy with anyone—Giana or Lou. When I got her on the phone, I told her to get on a train and come home pronto. She resisted at first, but she did it. I remember a tense conversation in a restaurant. God knows why we chose to talk it out there, as restaurants were usually very fraught territory. My perspective: for the past eighteen months, she had been in and out of residential treatment for anorexia and then bulimia, she was supposed to continue outpatient therapy, she was supposed to take classes in Philadelphia in the coming semester while we decided what to do about school more permanently, and the last thing she needed was to go chasing after a man. Her perspective: she wanted to be with him, she thought it was a good time to make a change to a new location, and the new boyfriend had promised they would get a puppy. A puppy, with the allergies and the asthma? She wanted to try it, wanted to test the years of allergy shots. Her last argument was that she was about to turn twenty-one. She could do it without permission, if it came to that. She prevailed, with the compromise that she would get into school immediately and would find an appropriate allergist and a therapist in Vermont.

I went to Vermont to visit her for the first time on Presidents' Day weekend. She had gotten herself into the community college up there, which, of course, I was happy about, and she was applying to the University of Vermont for the fall. I had booked a hotel overlooking Lake Champlain. Giana and the new snowboard instructor boyfriend (BF), who bore a striking resemblance to Prince William, met me for breakfast at the hotel. They were clearly in love, happy and affectionate and warm with each other. Giana looked radiant. In the lobby the first morning, there were signs warning guests about the severe wind chill—no outdoor activities that weekend. The BF said the mountain would be dangerous, and when we stepped outside to go to her apartment, I was assured that the sign was accurate. The wind and cold were stunning.

The apartment was basement level. I was taken aback by the general squalor, even with a new puppy, a terrible chewer, living there. I tried to clean, but it was pretty useless: the linoleum was cracking on the kitchen counter, the porcelain of the old tub was stained beyond cleanser, and no amount of vacuuming could clean those carpets. Abby, the puppy, was systematically ripping apart every piece of furniture in the place. It was also messy, odd for Giana, who was always obsessively tidy. I tried to be positive. I thought that maybe intense therapy during the active eating disorder and the medication had transformed her into someone more relaxed. Later, Giana took advantage of my being there to go out that evening with the BF while I stayed with Abby. I stopped trying to clean and sat down with a book, puppy asleep on my lap. She was a dark brindled boxer with floppy ears. At some point, Abby woke up and jumped to a bucket-shaped swivel chair next to the sofa. She began to run in a tight circle inside the chair, faster and faster, making the chair rotate. It was hilarious, but she did it for so long that I started to get worried that she would have apoplexy! Suddenly she stopped, flopped down, and in two seconds she was asleep and stayed that way until Giana came home.

I was still worried about Giana's weight and whether she was eating, and I took advantage of her absence to check out the fridge and the cupboards. There wasn't much food around, but she had never cooked, and she told me when I questioned her that they were mostly eating takeout and buying food on campus. The other thing that caught my attention was the marijuana or evidence of it—joint ends, baggies, matches, seeds—on almost every surface. As far as I knew, she had not been a regular user prior to this. I remember thinking that maybe it was good for her appetite.

I had smoked marijuana in my teens, along with everyone else. It was the sixties. I stopped at around age eighteen and never smoked again. I wasn't particularly opposed to it, didn't think of it as a terrible criminal act or a danger. I just thought of it as one more thing Giana didn't need to do. While Giana was growing up, some of our friends were marijuana users, and I made it clear to them that I didn't want it to happen in our house. My position was simply that I didn't want my kids to see adults doing it. I think some of our friends thought I was pretty uptight—a terrible thing to be in those days—but there it was: I didn't want it in the house. I was now surprised that it seemed so ubiquitous in Giana's apartment. When I asked, she said that the BF was a regular smoker. I didn't think much more about it at the time.

Over the next few years, I visited Giana frequently, still worried about a recurrence of the eating disorder. I remember one idyllic day that first summer when Abby was about ten months old. There was a dog beach on Lake Champlain, reached via a long gravel road. As we hiked toward the beach, Abby ran in and out of the high grass along the way, jumping, rolling, and making us laugh. I was surprised at how hot and humid it was, especially after experiencing Burlington in the winter. Giana looked healthy and fit in her bathing suit. After romping for a while with a Lab puppy on the beach, Abby delighted us both by jumping in and paddling out with us into deep, cool water.

The next fall when I visited, Giana and the BF were in a new apartment, and Giana was enrolled at the University of Vermont. The year at Rutgers, the courses at Temple in between residential treatment stays, and the semester at community college added up to a bit more than one year of transfer credits. Taking the advice of her doctors and therapists, Giana was carrying as light a load as possible for a full-time student and not working. Minimal stress was recommended. She declared as an English major, my daughter who loved to read.

The new apartment was just as messy as the last one, if not more so. I remember coming in for the first time just as Giana and the BF were getting out of bed—mattress on the floor, blankets and covers all over the place, clothes and shoes strewn about, and again, marijuana on every surface. Abby was chewing on a boot. Giana was busy going to class and, to my surprise, had begun swimming with the Vermont team after asking the coach if she could work out with them. When he learned about her previous times, he was all too happy to let her swim, but no scholarship, of course. I saw lots of evidence of the BF sleeping excessively and smoking weed and playing video games. I was worried, not so much about Giana and the marijuana but about the relationship. In retrospect, I should have worried about the weed.

What does the evidence say? Is marijuana a "gateway" to more dangerous substances? The answers are "sometimes" and "more research is needed." It is important to note that most marijuana users do not progress to opioids and other drugs such as cocaine. However, here is the guidance from the latest brief on this subject, titled "Is Marijuana a Gateway Drug?" by NIDA. "Some research suggests that marijuana use is likely to precede use of other licit and illicit substances and the development of addiction to other substances." So while it is likely that most marijuana users won't progress to "harder" drugs, many people who use those drugs initially used marijuana. The report notes that tobacco, alcohol, and marijuana may act as gateways among people who, for a variety of reasons such as genetics, environment, and mental health issues, are already at risk. There is evidence that "alcohol and nicotine also prime the brain for a heightened response to other drugs and are, like marijuana, also typically used before a person progresses to other, more harmful substances."

Many, many people smoke marijuana and do not progress to heroin. However, someone like Giana, already in treatment for serious mental health issues, including an obsessive coping behavior such as an eating disorder, is at a much higher risk than those who do not have this history. I should have been more concerned, especially after she moved on from this BF and the association with marijuana continued.

At some point she met a guy at the dog park. I didn't know anything about him until one day when she was in Philly; I heard her talking on the phone in a flirty way with someone I realized wasn't the BF. I tried to ask her about it, but she was evasive. Next thing we knew, the BF had burst into the guy's apartment and punched him. There were holes in walls and an angry landlord.

What's all this?

Lou had to sort out the legal aftermath. My concern about Giana's behavior in romantic relationships deepened. One of her sisters said that she enjoyed the drama, and as soon as a relationship grew calm, she made sure that drama happened. Pretty accurate, and a worrisome foreshadowing of the years to come. I was concerned about this latest boyfriend, who, I finally figured out, made his living as a weed dealer, supplemented by a trust fund.

I continued to visit Giana frequently. At some point in a locker room or a hotel room, I saw the new, large tattoo on her lower back. It was a design with the number twenty-one in the middle. It was right at that time when girls were wearing low-cut jeans and thongs to show off their lower-back tattoos. I am not a tattoo fan and I was not happy, but it was done and I knew that I should pick my battles. "Why twenty-one?" I asked.

"My birthday, of course," she replied.

Celeste and Louisa both visited Giana in Vermont several times. I just looked through a picture album of Giana's time in Vermont that has a series with each of them—big girls now, pictures of them in bars and in bikinis on the lake beach. In one set of pictures Giana and Celeste are with a bunch of people jumping off a cliff into Lake Champlain. I'm so glad I didn't know about that at the time! Giana had always been close to both her sisters, although she spent more time with Louisa because of the nine-year age difference with Celeste. Still, I can remember times when Giana was a preschooler that the three of them played for hours in Barbie Heaven—several dozen dolls, clothes, tiny pocketbooks and shoes, the Barbie Dream House, the Barbie Corvette, the Barbie Kitchen, the Barbie horses and dogs, and the Barbie Salon. Giana wrote about her sisters in her second-grade journal: "Having big sisters is harobol [*sic*]. They always boss you around and you always get into fights. But sometimes it's nice because they play games with you and they babysit you and stuff like that."

In her junior year at Vermont, I remember being on the pool deck watching Giana explain to the other girls on the team why she had to stop swimming with them. The stress of competition had kicked in, and she recognized that her anxiety was building. I was proud of her for taking the steps needed to maintain her well-being. She remained a volunteer manager and supported the team at home meets.

Sometimes I thought that Burlington was good for her: the slower pace, the long winters (like me, she always loved winter), the dog culture she had adopted, the more laid-back environment. I never saw anybody there hurtling to work in heels and hose at eight in the morning as I did at home. It seemed safe for her, and I wondered if she should stay. How ironic that Vermont later became an epicenter of the heroin epidemic.

Still, at a certain point during her time in Vermont, even with the ongoing boyfriend drama, I relaxed. When she moved into her own apartment—no boyfriend—tidiness returned. No further recurrence of the eating disorder. I remember thinking as her graduation approached, *Wow! Nightmare is over*. I really wasn't worried about her—she was doing well in school, she was communicative, and the dog didn't seem to be sending her to the ER with asthma attacks.

What was I missing?

~

Giana didn't attend any graduation exercises at the University of Vermont. I understood. I didn't attend mine either; it had seemed like a chore when graduating from a school along with thousands of others, and years later than expected. Easier to just pick up your diploma and move on.

She came back to Philly in early 2005, completely unsure of what she was going to do. She and her dog, Abby, moved into the family home with her dad, and she started waitressing. She toyed around with a lot of ideas, some of which involved graduate school: journalism, teaching high school English, becoming a librarian. None of them seemed quite right. "I want someone to pay me to read," she said to me.

"Well," I said, "you could try working for a publisher or a literary agency—lots of business involved there, though. And lots of interaction with cranky writers and difficult editors. And you probably will have to move to New York." So she waitressed, went to the gym, took Abby to the dog park every day, and read. She had some friends, not too many and not many very close, but she socialized a bit, worked full time and took care of her dog, and seemed, if not happy, at least content. Eventually she moved into an apartment with a high school girlfriend. She spent a lot of time with her brother, who had recently returned, married, from a long time in Japan. There were more terrible boyfriends. She was twenty-six.

In the fall of 2006, Louisa turned thirty. She had gone to Colorado for a graduate school internship and was still living there. A friend agreed to let her use his place on the west coast of Mexico for a five-day birthday vacation. Giana flew there to join her sister and a few others. I had already planned to take my mother away to visit family for a few days over the same weekend. We agreed that I would take Abby for boarding at the place where she sometimes went for doggy day care. Abby loved that place, and we didn't give it a second thought.

The next morning, as I was waking up in a hotel three and a half hours from Philly, my cell phone rang. That morning the boarding facility had made the inexcusable mistake of letting several dogs out of their cages to eat at the same time, and another dog had attacked Abby to get at her food. They decided to take Abby to the University of Pennsylvania vet emergency room, just as a precaution, they said. A little while later a vet from there called me to tell me that Abby would need surgery, and they couldn't promise that she would survive. The dog had punctured Abby's lungs with its teeth and the risk of infection was high. I was shocked and frightened. I decided to leave my mother with our cousins, and I drove home, straight to the vet hospital. On the way I had several calls with the vet and also with the business office of the hospital. I put down a big deposit and they prepared for surgery.

I loved Abby and was very upset, but more than that, I was worried about how Giana would react if things didn't go well. While there had been no recurrence of her eating disorder, she was still seeing a psychiatrist and was medicated for depression and anxiety. She was fragile. I called Celeste, another dog lover, and told her what was going on, and she joined me at the hospital. James came too. We all agreed that I needed to try to reach Giana.

Abby was in surgery for a very long time. Finally, as night fell, the surgeon came out to talk with us. Abby had come through the surgery, but she wasn't out of the woods. The next few days were critical. Celeste and I went up to see Abby; she was still under anesthesia with tubes coming out of everywhere. She was curled on some blankets in a crate on the floor, in a room with several other critically ill dogs. I went home and lay on the sofa watching TV, totally unable to sleep.

Late that evening, I got through to Giana, who immediately began making arrangements to fly home. When she arrived the next day, we went straight to the hospital. Giana sat by the crate where Abby was beginning to stir, sluggish from pain medication. She sat there every minute she was permitted over the next few days. In doing so, she was able to observe how this critical care unit operated, and she realized that the place depended upon what the hospital called veterinary nurses. Talking with one of them, Giana learned that Penn had a collaboration with another college to train the nurses. The classes were taught at the other school, and the nurses—or techs, as some other facilities call them—did a semester interning at Penn's primary hospital and another semester at Penn's large animal facility. It was a two- to three-year program, depending upon what credits you brought with you and how many credits you could take in a semester.

Abby had led Giana to her calling.

A few months after her surgery, Abby had recovered and, except for the big scar jagging across her chest and abdomen, was much the same as always. Giana had applied to the vet nursing program and been accepted. So over the next two years, Giana went to school full time, waitressed part time, and spent time in the gym. She was so busy that I didn't spend as much time with her as usual, but my help with Abby increased, at least until JM, the pathway to opioids, came along. She had met him in the gym, and when her roommate moved out, he conveniently moved in. His single redeeming quality was that he was great with Abby.

In the early spring of 2008, Giana called me one day at work to say that she was on her way to Penn's emergency room with Abby. She said that Abby was increasingly lethargic and not behaving at all normally. I told her I'd meet her there. Giana knew enough at this point to understand when something might be serious. When I arrived, they had done some tests on Abby, and Giana was just sitting down with the doctor. He gave us the terrible cancer diagnosis. Giana immediately broke down in sobs so convulsive that the doctor left the room for a few minutes to give her a chance to compose herself. Abby was only seven.

The cancer was in her lungs, and surgery was not recommended. The vet explained that she could be treated for a while with low doses of chemotherapy. It is typical veterinary practice not to use chemotherapy the way we do with humans, with massive doses that may kill the cancer but also make the dog very sick. The idea is to prolong life, with good quality of life, for as long as possible. The dog, after all, is not looking into its future and contemplating death.

Giana and I both took Abby to chemotherapy, depending on our work schedules. Abby would stay several hours. She never seemed agitated about going, and the most resistance we got would be a plaintive look as they took her back, communicating, "Why aren't you coming with me? I like my people with me!" I recall being with Giana and Abby in the dog park while she was on chemo. She wasn't as frisky as she had previously been, but she ran and she waded into the pond. No one who hadn't known her previously would have thought anything was wrong. Quality of life: good.

Until it wasn't. Three months into the chemo, Giana called me at work and said she was taking Abby in and feared the worst. She said that over the past day or two, when Abby went outside, she lay down in the grass with no energy for even a short walk. Inside she was sleeping almost all the time, with no interest in her toys. I rushed to the hospital and was taken back to a room where Giana and JM were sitting on the floor with Abby. Giana had been right; the tumors were growing, and soon enough Abby would be unable to breathe properly. We were all crying. I remember suggesting that maybe we didn't need to do it right now, maybe there was still some time. Giana replied that it was better for the vet to do it now. She didn't want Abby to experience any panic or pain. About forty-five minutes later, she told the vet she was ready. She sat on the floor with Abby's head cradled in her lap. I sat nearby in a chair, bending over and stroking Abby's back, memorizing the pattern of her brindled fur. It only took a few minutes.

We left with promises that they would take Abby's footprint and would call us when we could pick up her ashes. We were almost out the door, Giana sobbing, when she turned around and went back, saying that she hadn't had enough time. She cuddled

Abby's body for another ten minutes or so, and then we left.

If there had been any chance of turning away from pain-quelling drug use, I think it was lost that day.

~

September 19, 2017: My sweet Giana, I have good news. I took Jade to the vet yesterday, just shy of her ninth birthday, and she's doing very well! It's always hard for me to go there, that place where you used to work, the last job you held, where you fell apart. Many people who were there then are still there. Everyone is very polite to me, very professional. No one mentions you unless I do. When they print out my receipt, your name is still on the account.

In my basement is a bin filled with your scrubs. Navy blue scrubs.

But I think Jade is better off continuing to go there, even if it's hard for me. You know how agitated she can get about certain things. When we go there, she is both eager and scared. I always wonder whether she thinks she'll see you there, whether she still associates that place with you. I drove by the old dog park recently, where we used to take her, where your bench is, and she got very excited in the car. I never take her there now. When I go there, which is rare, I just want to sit quietly on your bench. We go to other parks where the memories don't pierce.

But back to Jade. When we got into the examining room, she was whining and tried to sit on my lap. Silly dog! Then when the vet opened the door, she scooted under a chair and tried to hide. She's much the same as she has always been, since you rescued her and brought her home after her stay in the emergency room where you were working. Remember her, five weeks old, tiny little thing? We could hold her in two hands. But she was plucky even then.

She looks like a much younger dog, so lean and muscular. She still weighs fifty-nine pounds, so you see how well I am caring for her. James and I take her to the park every day to run, and she gets long walks too. You know she loves table food, and she gets some, but her staple is the dry dog food that she won't overeat. It took three of us to hold her still for her shots. The only giveaways to her age are the gray hairs that are starting to accumulate on her face and, if you know her well, that she sleeps more.

Lucky girl, you have escaped the pain of eventually letting her go, leaving that to me.

Giana with her beloved dog, Abby

Chapter Seven

May 2012: I was at work late on Memorial Day, preparing for summer camp. It had been a busy social weekend, and I wanted to be organized for the upcoming week. It was early evening, and as always, I felt a deep sense of satisfaction being in our large renovated factory building alone, getting things done without interruption. Sometimes it seemed that during the regular workday, my primary task was managing interruptions. We were preparing for our summer programs, which provided day camp and summer employment to thousands of young people in Philly and Camden. I was out in our multipurpose room, checking on the progress staff had made sorting games and supplies to be sent out to the camp sites. My cell phone rang where I had left it on my desk, but I didn't make it back to the office area in time to answer. I listened to the message from Giana. I had to listen again, because the information was so difficult to process. She was in a drug treatment center, a facility called Keystone. She said something like, "There's a lot more going on than you know about, Mom." She said she would call me again.

What's all this?

I wasn't going to wait for another phone call. I immediately googled Keystone and called them. All they would tell me was that she was there, but no details. Of course I argued, accustomed to getting information when I wanted it. But that's all I could get; her age and HIPAA laws protected her.

I thought back to brunch with her earlier in the weekend. We'd sat outside on a soft, moist, early summer day. She kept her sunglasses on the whole time but looked lovely. Not underweight, skin glowing, long shiny hair loose. We talked about her job at an emergency and surgical animal hospital. She had recently been assisting in ophthalmologic surgeries and was finding it interesting and challenging. Other than that, she spoke only when prompted by me, but that wasn't so unusual—she had been a quiet child and was a quiet adult. When we left the restaurant and were on the sidewalk, I remember asking, "Are you okay?"

"Just tired," she replied. I didn't believe her, but I didn't push. I never pushed enough. I stood and watched as she went to her car, and I remember seeing her turn and wave at me through the back window as the car went by down the street. I relive that moment all the time now—the beginning of saying goodbye?

I was confused, worried, but not exactly panicked. She was somewhere safe, and she had called.

But why hadn't she told me before, the many times I asked if she was okay? Was the shame I came to understand so crushing? Did ambivalence about being well interfere?

Lou, from whom I was now divorced, was in Florida and had been down there for a while, expecting Giana to join him because her great-aunt was ill and likely dying. Auntie had no children, and Giana was her favorite niece. She had come to visit from Florida the day after Giana was born, and from there a bond seemed to form. Over the years, Giana went to Florida to visit a number of times. Giana had been putting her father off for the past few months as Auntie got sicker, saying she couldn't leave work. Her aunt died a day before Giana checked herself in to Keystone. Related? Later when I visited her at Keystone, she told me that she knew she wasn't stable enough to travel and didn't know what else to do except what she did. It was a good choice that should have been made long before it was.

I recalled Louisa's wedding two years earlier on a beach far from home. Giana's behavior was very odd during that trip. She did the duty a sister is supposed to do: helping Louisa with preparations, arranging flowers, fussing over hair and dress. She went surfing with everybody. But a lot of the time she was inaccessible and grim. I heard from Louisa that she sought out a friendly local to sell her some marijuana. *Really?* I thought. But Giana didn't drink, and almost everyone else made use of the beachfront bar in the evenings while we were there, so I let it go. It didn't seem so different. I also wanted the trip to be about Louisa—it was, after all, her wedding.

A few days after the wedding, a group went zip-lining. Giana came back ashen; she had been so terrified that Celeste had to coax her to continue. This was so unlike her. Although cautious, she had never been fearful of heights, the child who at ten had run up the Eiffel Tower while Louisa and I cowered on the first platform, paralyzed; Giana, the one who skipped down the narrow path of the Grand Canyon, leaving me breathless with fear; Giana, the one who a few years earlier was eager to ski the double black diamond; Giana, the one who jumped off cliffs with Celeste into Lake Champlain. When our flight home after the wedding was delayed due to weather, she was anxious to the point of hysterics. Celeste had to literally hold her close to calm her down. She had just started a job and said she was afraid of not getting back in time. Later I realized that she was afraid of running out of her drug supply.

The day after Giana checked in to Keystone, I called Lou in Florida. Of course he was shocked. And angry. In the end, Celeste and Greg went down and helped Lou get through the funeral. At the time I felt, *You should have been there, Giana. Your siblings are always stepping in for you.* This response shows how little I understood about the challenges she was facing. I don't think she fully understood either.

I visited her at Keystone about five days later, after she had completed detox. I remember that they kept my handbag at the check-in desk, protecting her from me, in theory. I was directed to the dining area, institutional but small. I sat and waited for her. I looked around at the other family members, waiting—some fidgeting with anxiety, others looking bored—for their child or their sister or their somebody. When Giana came in, I stood up, and she hugged me, stifling a sob. I don't remember precisely what she said, but the general information was this: she had been injecting a drug called Nubain for several years. Nubain? Nalbuphine is a semisynthetic opioid used commercially as an analgesic under a variety of trade names, including Nubain. Apparently at the time it was the drug of choice for bodybuilders; visions surfaced of Giana and JM, the unemployed bodybuilder boyfriend. JM had initially supplied her with the Nubain, until she started going straight to the dealer, another bodybuilder. One dealer for the Nubain, another dealer for the weed. All of a sudden, her inability to live on her pretty decent income made sense.

However, what I remember most clearly from that visit to Keystone was the change in her tone when she told me about the new boyfriend. A new boyfriend, after a week? "I met someone; there, you can see him through the window," she said, and directed my gaze out to the smoking area. "He treats me like a princess," she said, her voice sliding toward a little girl lisp.

I remember that I forced her to look at me and said something like, "You aren't here to meet guys. This is not the time or place. What are you doing?"

And at this point, I didn't even know about the general prohibition against relationships during the first year of recovery and the major prohibition against forming a relationship with another user in rehab. The more she told me, the worse it got. Sent to Keystone from jail or court. Nine years younger than she was. I remember saying to her, "He may be a nice kid, but not for you. And not now. Right now, you need to focus on yourself."

And then the mantra I had repeated to her many times over the years, confronted with her perplexing choice of boyfriends: You have to feel comfortable with yourself, by yourself. You can't rely on them, not to make you feel okay, and not to take care of you. And remember, people choose someone they feel worthy of.

When she was thinking clearly and being reflective, Giana was well aware of this issue. In her journal a few months after this, she wrote: "I am addicted to men for sure. I lost myself in my first serious relationship and probably have never been the same. I always turned myself over to the person wholeheartedly and felt that if I was loved by them, then I had a purpose. When relationships ended, I was always devastated and deeply depressed. I felt like I had no sense of self, and without that person I was lost."

Because Giana's individual therapy in all of the rehabs was infrequent, this issue was never adequately explored. There were various groups at various facilities where relationships were addressed, but both because Giana didn't function well in groups and because the groups were in general poorly organized and facilitated, little progress resulted from her participation in group after group.

After my visit at Keystone, I was asked to come back a few days later for a "family session." One family session does not family therapy make. Giana's insurance company, which had referred her to Keystone, approved fourteen days, or perhaps she told them that she could only stay fourteen days because of work; I don't know which. So with the time up in a few days, we talked largely about her discharge plan, which amounted to ninety Alcoholics Anonymous (AA) or Narcotics Anonymous (NA) sessions in ninety days and weekly therapy with someone they recommended. Oh, and avoid stress.

At no time did the counselor discuss medication, although there was medication, FDA approved and in use at this time. I had no idea, and I don't think Giana did either. A full-time, stressful job, a meeting every day, and a new therapist an hour's drive away? Why not go back to her former therapist, who had treated her during her eating disorder and was much closer than an hour's drive, I asked. They wanted her to see someone whose practice was focused on substance use. There was no discussion in this hour of "family therapy," of Giana's diagnosed mental health issues, her medication for them, or her psychiatrist. I remember wondering whether a decade of smoking marijuana and a few years of using Nubain could be addressed by two inpatient weeks, a meeting every day, and a weekly hour of therapy. *But these people must know what they're doing*, I thought. While waiting in the lobby, I had examined a license hanging on the wall in a frame. Giana's insurance company was paying them—would an insurance company, focused on their bottom line, pay for something they knew to be ineffective? And I was reassured by her resolve—hadn't she contacted the insurance company and checked herself in?

> *My response was indicative of the person I was then, a believer that problems can almost always be solved, especially if one finds the right formula. But what I should have done was to launch full force into understanding substance use disorder and its treatment. I have thought many times since that if she had been diagnosed with cancer, I would have been all over it.*

When I was leaving that day, a fight broke out, and I had to be escorted out of the facility by a different door than the one where I'd entered. Giana told me that the fight was among guys who were there on public insurance and that those patients, her new crush included, were kept in a different part of the facility and had a different program than the private insurance patients.

I questioned her about that; did she mean patients on public insurance or patients who were there because of court order? Both? It didn't sound legal, separating people because of their type of payment. Would that happen if people were there to be treated for something else, glaucoma or diverticulitis or whatever; would they receive different treatment based on their insurance type? But I had to leave, and I forgot all about it.

On day thirteen of Giana's stay at Keystone, I was in the car with my mother, driving her home from a hair appointment. My mother had stopped driving a year earlier, and we had all become her chauffeurs. Giana called. She had left treatment earlier that day, a day before she should have, AMA (against medical advice). I suspected it was because the new boyfriend, M, had been discharged, which Giana later confirmed. Of course, Keystone wouldn't have called me to tell me Giana left; she was thirty-two. I barely said a word, just made monosyllabic responses barely audible over the Natalie Cole CD playing in the car. The last thing I wanted was for my eighty-seven-year-old mother, who loved Giana so much, to know about any of this.

~

What was wrong with her?

I was blindsided by Giana's drug use. I knew something was wrong, had felt it for a long time, had tried to respectfully ask her if something was troubling her, the careful way a parent asks a probing personal question to an adult child who has completed her education and is working. Her history of mental health and eating disorder issues gave me a bit more license, perhaps, but I was too passive. I greatly regret not being more assertive and demanding information. I know now an earlier intervention and a medically sound approach might have made a difference, especially before she turned to heroin.

What if I had gone through her stuff one of the many times she asked me to stop by her apartment to feed the guinea pigs or walk the dogs? What if I had gone through her stuff and found the Nubain bottles and the syringes?

Like many other family members who are suddenly confronted by serious drug use, I had no idea what we were facing. I wish now, every single day, that I had dropped many other "priorities" in my life and delved more deeply. I was trying to achieve positive outcomes in my work, I was investing energy in being a grandmother, I was involved in a relationship, and I was trying to be a doting but unobtrusive parent to grown children. Something had to give if I were to provide the support and time that Giana was going to need, but I recognized that too late. I don't know if this could have saved her, but I wouldn't feel the regrets I have now that I waited too long to understand and that I believed "experts" who, it turns out, were part of a broken, outdated, ineffective response.

What was wrong with her? The *Diagnostic and Statistical Manual of Mental Disorders* (DSM) 5th edition, released in May 2013, uses the term "substance use disorder" (SUD) to name and describe what was formerly called either abuse or dependence. Subcategories are used to define specifics for alcohol, tobacco, opioids, and so forth. OUD is the abbreviated term for opioid use disorder. (Opiates are drugs derived from opium. At one time "opioids" referred to synthetic opiates only, but currently the term opioid is used for the entire family of opiates, including natural, synthetic, and semisynthetic). Symptoms of opioid use disorder include the inability to control or reduce use and continued use despite interference with major obligations or social functioning. This doesn't mean that the user doesn't *want* to stop; it signals that the user is *unable* to stop, despite all the associated negative consequences. Because this behavior is so exasperating, it's very hard to understand unless one thinks of OUD as a mental illness, a medical condition, not a choice.

The DSM uses a set of symptoms to classify whether the use disorder is mild, moderate, or severe. Based on these, at the time of her voluntary admission to Keystone, Giana's substance use disorder had been moderate but was quickly becoming severe, interfering with her life in multiple ways. I was stunned when she revealed she had used Nubain subcutaneously during the two years of vet school but managed to complete the program early and with excellent grades. She told me her initial use coincided with Abby's death. But she turned to intravenous use, either when she began working in the field or shortly thereafter, possibly because of another failed relationship and an accident that resulted in an opioid prescription. Those with the most severe substance use disorders are often characterized as having an addiction, and that was where Giana was clearly headed when she entered Keystone, although she had not yet begun to use heroin.

Addiction is now considered a chronic relapsing disease. The 2016 Surgeon General's report says, "Research has shown that substance use disorders are similar in course, management, and outcome to other chronic illnesses, such as hypertension, diabetes, and asthma . . . it is possible to adopt the same type of chronic care management approach to the treatment of substance use disorders as is now used to manage most other chronic illnesses." In some cases complete recovery may occur, but more often, especially with opioid addiction, continuing care—maybe lifelong care—is necessary.

In no setting was this ever explained in this way to Giana or to me. While some treatment programs used terms like "chronic disease," and all the rehabs paid lots of attention to relapse through lectures and worksheets, nowhere were we counseled that her disorder was fundamentally a medical issue for which she would need lifelong medically planned care. And absolutely nowhere was it explained that the most effective treatment, based on the evidence from rigorous studies, is medication-assisted treatment (MAT), which combines medication with psychosocial and behavioral therapies delivered by highly trained professionals.

Apart from medication used in detox, the idea that medication could and should be part of ongoing treatment was never discussed at Keystone or at her next stop on the rehab journey, Valley Forge Medical Center. Yet at that time, there were three different medications approved by the FDA. The first, which I vaguely knew about, was methadone. What I remembered about methadone was that people went to clinics daily to get it, which is true. Tightly controlled, methadone can only be dispensed at clinics approved and regulated by the Substance Abuse and Mental Health Service Administration (SAMHSA), an arm of the federal Department of Health and Human Services. Methadone is a slow-acting opioid agonist, which means that it acts like other agonists, including heroin and oxycodone, by bonding to the brain's opioid receptors. However, because it is taken orally, is slow-acting, and remains in the body for a long time, it is effective in reducing cravings and has allowed many people to function relatively normally, if properly dosed. According to a 2014 SAMHSA brief entitled "Adult Drug Courts and Medication-Assisted Treatment for Opioid Dependence," "It does not produce the same euphoric effects as heroin, morphine, and other full agonists." As such, "Methadone both reduces cravings for illicit opioids and prevents withdrawal symptoms, enabling people taking it to lead productive and fulfilling lives." Although I didn't know much, I carried some of the stigmatized attitudes so common about methadone, that it's just a replacement drug that is for people who can't get it together and remain abstinent.

So, what if, upon leaving Keystone, Giana had been referred to a methadone clinic? Wouldn't I prefer that my daughter take a daily dose of methadone and be alive and functioning, instead of gaz-

ing at the urn containing her ashes and wondering what might have been? What if I had figured this out while she was at Keystone instead of following their discharge recommendation of ninety meetings in ninety days?

Buprenorphine is another medication used to treat opioid dependence and is now considered to be the most effective one. It is most commonly used in a combination product called Suboxone, which also contains naloxone (which is the ingredient in the now well-known emergency overdose drug commercially called Narcan). Unlike methadone, buprenorphine is a partial agonist. Naloxone is an antagonist. Together, they reduce cravings and withdrawal symptoms. Suboxone is usually taken as a film placed under the tongue and can be prescribed by a doctor approved through federal criteria. In 2016 an implantable form of buprenorphine that releases medication for six months was approved by the FDA, and in 2017 a monthly shot was approved. Obviously these were not available when Giana was alive, but no facility offered her the Suboxone film. Numerous studies have shown buprenorphine to be effective as a long-term maintenance therapy.

The third approved medication is naltrexone, an opioid antagonist; it blocks the effect of heroin and other opioids, as well as alcohol—a person cannot get high while on it. Naltrexone was originally approved to treat alcoholism and later approved for use with opioids. As with methadone and Suboxone film, one drawback of naltrexone in pill form is that its effectiveness relies upon the patient taking the medication as directed—that is, the patient's compliance—which conflicts with the definition of OUD explained earlier, that the user is *unable* to stop despite all the associated negative consequences. In 2010 the FDA approved an injectable form of naltrexone called Vivitrol, which is given once a month. No special protocols are necessary for a doctor to prescribe and administer Vivitrol. At this point, there is far less research on the long-term efficacy of Vivitrol than exists for methadone and buprenorphine, although it is certainly the medication of choice for alcoholism. While it is not clear whether the reduction of cravings some opioid users on Vivitrol report is physical or psychological or both, research on this continues. Naltrexone is, however, the remedy of choice for those holding the mistaken belief that methadone and buprenorphine simply substitute one addiction for another.

What if Valley Forge, which used methadone for her detox, had kept Giana on a maintenance dose and discharged her with a referral to a methadone clinic? What if the Malvern Institute had allowed Giana to participate in their program, taking the Suboxone that her psychiatrist recommended to dull the cravings that kept her from being more focused on her recovery? What if, from the day of her admission to Caron, medication-assisted treatment had been a pillar of their treatment program, just like the long list of other interventions, from cognitive behavioral therapy (CBT) to mindfulness meditation, which weren't a choice? Or what if she had been given a shot of Vivitrol before leaving Caron and continuing monthly shots were part of the protocol of My First Year, an aftercare service that we paid Caron for? Here's what: she would likely not have died in the next treatment program, The Rose House, three weeks after her Caron discharge. She would still have had a chance to get well.

As stated previously, this was all known by the time of Giana's first residential treatment stay in June 2012. The following is from a July 2012 peer-reviewed study published in the PubMed Central of the US National Library of Medicine, part of the National Institutes of Health: "Treatment for opiate addiction requires long-term management. Behavioral interventions alone have extremely poor outcomes, with more than 80 percent of patients returning to drug use. . . . Results indicate that maintenance medication provides the best opportunity for patients to achieve recovery from opiate addiction. Extensive literature and systematic review show that maintenance treatment with either methadone or buprenorphine is associated with retention in treatment, reduction in illicit opiate use, decreased craving, and improved social function. Oral naltrexone is ineffective in treating opiate addiction, but recent studies using extended release naltrexone injections have shown promise."

Why this refusal, then, among these licensed and very expensive treatment providers, to embrace medication, when the evidence then and now clearly demonstrates its effectiveness over treatment that doesn't include medication? Simply put, the answer is the legacy of Alcoholics Anonymous. Most currently operating private rehabs have grown from programs that treated alcoholism and used AA's 12 Steps as their method. In that world, using medication as treatment is disparaged as substituting one drug for another. Although AA doesn't take a formal position on medication assisted treatment, many AA meetings shun people who are using medication to assist recovery. NA, however, is explicitly opposed to MAT. While both AA and NA may now use the lingo that substance use disorder is a disease, they do not see it as a chronic disease like asthma, diabetes, and hypertension. They still see it, in the AA tradition, as a moral failing that causes one to have character defects—a huge contradiction that leaves patients and their families confused about what is wrong, causing them to ask: *Is it a disease or just a matter of will? How can recovering from a disease be a matter of will, cured by acknowledging one's powerlessness over it?*

One of the things Giana received at Caron over a year after her discharge from Keystone was a handout entitled "Checklist of Flaws and Assets" listing about 120 "character defects" on the left side of a column and the opposite asset on the other side. Examples: apprehensive, afraid vs. calm, courageous; enabling vs. setting boundaries, tough love; loud vs. tasteful, quiet.

Maybe if you are tasteful and quiet, you'll have a better shot at recovery than if you are loud.

The implication here is that patient behavior and attitude is a determinant both of how one becomes addicted and how a person addresses his or her addiction. In fact, there are many other diseases that are impacted by patient behavior. A November 2017 article by Mike Stobbe that appeared in the *Philadelphia Inquirer* reported on a study done by the American Cancer Society that concluded that 45 percent of cancer deaths could be attributed to behavior such as "exposure to sun, not eating enough fruits and vegetables, drinking alcohol and, most importantly, smoking." The article also stated that obesity "was associated with 60 percent of uterine cancers and one-third of liver cancers." While medical care should always include instruction and support for healthy habits, can we imagine telling these patients that they have characters defects and that their illness results from a lack of willpower—and therefore, they will not be treated with the most recently proven effective strategies, such as medication, but by participating in talk groups with others who have the same character defects?

~

Even though I knew little about addiction and recovery after Giana's thirteen-day stay at Keystone, I did wonder how a discharge with the prescription to attend "ninety meetings in ninety days" would cure her, especially after I attended the first meeting with her. This meeting was held at a neighborhood hospital in Philadelphia, less than ten minutes from my house. A close friend of Giana's and I went with her, for support. There was no signage indicating where the meeting was, so we ended up asking a custodian who was outside sweeping up. He pointed us to a warehouse-like building near the hospital dumpsters, and we went inside. It was set up like an auditorium. There was a person sitting in front and one person sitting in the "audience" section. Two or three more people entered after us. The person in front introduced himself with the typical, "My name is X, and I am an addict," followed by the others in the room. People were asked to say how long they had been sober: one person said a day. He didn't look good. The moderator read for about fifteen minutes from AA/NA materials and then asked someone else in the room to read. Sadly, the person who volunteered was barely literate, and what might have been a few minutes turned into a painful ten as she attempted to sound out words or supply a word that seemed to fit the context. There was a brief discussion during which the only people who spoke were the moderator and a guy way in the back who said he'd been sober for thirty-three years. Giana didn't say a word. The moderator reviewed some handouts, and we left. I was perplexed and discouraged. Certainly not treatment, this didn't even qualify as support.

Since the 12 Steps of AA/NA hover over and simmer under Giana's journey through addiction, treatment, and death, they are supplied here.

The 12 Steps became the standard for treating alcohol use disorder in the late 1930s and 1940s when alcoholism was assumed to be a moral failing, and the medical community had little to offer as an alternative to AA. It was also very cost effective, since the primary qualification of the "personnel" was that they were recovering alcoholics themselves for whom AA had been successful. The initial model of an anonymous fellowship of people supporting each other's abstinence remains. There are many thousands of meetings taking place around the globe every day. However, along the way, alcohol rehab facilities were founded and used the AA 12-Step program as their basis. And then, the rehab industry extended the model to treatment for all substance use disorders and eventually applied it to compulsive gambling and sexual behaviors.

The AA 12 Steps and the NA 12 Steps differ only in that the words alcohol/alcoholic are replaced by addiction/addict. Otherwise, the steps are identical. Here they are:

Twelve Steps of Narcotics Anonymous

1. We admitted that we were powerless over our addiction, that our lives had become unmanageable.
2. We came to believe that a Power greater than ourselves could restore us to sanity.
3. We made a decision to turn our will and our lives over to the care of God *as we understood Him*.
4. We made a searching and fearless moral inventory of ourselves.
5. We admitted to God, to ourselves, and to another human being the exact nature of our wrongs.
6. We were entirely ready to have God remove all these defects of character.
7. We humbly asked Him to remove our shortcomings.
8. We made a list of all persons we had harmed, and became willing to make amends to them all.
9. We made direct amends to such people wherever possible, except when to do so would injure them or others.
10. We continued to take personal inventory and when we were wrong promptly admitted it.
11. We sought through prayer and meditation to improve our conscious contact with God *as we understood Him*,

praying only for knowledge of His will for us and the power to carry that out.

12. Having had a spiritual awakening as a result of these steps, we tried to carry this message to addicts, and to practice these principles in all our affairs.

What an empire has been built on those 12 Steps! What a transformation from what began as an anonymous group of people trying to support one another to stop drinking. Of course, the anonymous self-help groups do still exist, and many people find them helpful as recovery support. But now the vast majority of rehab programs incorporate the 12 Steps in some way and use materials based on them. In addition to the AA and NA basic texts, all the rehabs where Giana sought help used a lot of materials produced by the Hazelden Foundation (now Hazelden Betty Ford). Hazelden is over sixty-five years old and pioneered what was called the Minnesota model. Simply put, the model was a contrast to the prevailing approaches to alcoholism at the time and advocated for alcoholics living together in a supportive community. From that simple beginning, Hazelden has grown into a large institution with seventeen treatment sites, the largest publishing house of material on addiction and recovery, and a variety of educational programs.

Many of the materials Giana left behind from various treatment facilities are copies of Hazelden publications that were recopied numerous times. For example, among Giana's Valley Forge Medical Center files is a 1985 article published by Hazelden called "Stinking Thinking," a Hazelden pamphlet called "King Baby" from 1986, and several chapters of a 1977 Hazelden publication called "The Foundation of Recovery" about the 12 Steps.

There are a number of other sources for 12-Step materials as well, of course. However, none of the many handouts Giana left behind are recent. One concern here is that an enormous amount of research has taken place in the past thirty years, and new approaches to treatment have developed as a result. When I see the distorted print of materials that have been recopied over and over, some with evidence of past highlighting, underlining, and even margin notes, I have to wonder whether treatment center employees have kept up with that research.

Chapter Eight

Summer 2012: After her discharge from Keystone, early in June, Giana went immediately back to work full time and overtime. I felt as if I was walking on eggshells, constantly anxious, constantly asking her questions about whether she was going to meetings, whether she was seeing the therapist, whether she had cravings, whether she was okay. She usually said everything was fine. I didn't really believe her, but I wanted to.

She was supposed to be staying with a good friend for a while, thinking that being alone was not a smart idea. I agreed. Her apartment was twenty or thirty minutes from my house, his house about forty-five. The result of this and our work schedules was that we saw each other only about once a week initially, but I called her at least once a day.

Summer was always a very busy time for me at work. We ran about twenty day camps in Philly and Camden, as well as a large summer youth employment program for teens. This was in addition to our AmeriCorps program, our daycare center and Head Start programs, continual grant writing, and various other things. As soon as the summer programs were launched and functioning well, usually by the second week of July, planning for the fall began. I loved my job, but now I think I should probably have left it at this point to support Giana and, truthfully, to monitor Giana. But I couldn't easily do that financially, as I was not yet eligible for Medicare or Social Security benefits.

One day in early July, I called her several times without an answer. Feeling panicked, I called the guy she had been staying with, who informed me that she had gone back to her apartment two weeks earlier. I was furious and sent her a 911 text. She called me immediately, and I let loose on her for not telling me. She said that she hadn't wanted to worry me but that this friend was romantically interested in her and she couldn't reciprocate, and that their dogs weren't getting along. She decided it was best just to go home. I was angry and suspicious. I asked her if the new rehab boyfriend, M, was there with her, and she said sometimes. I wasn't happy about that either, but I thought there was little I could do about it. She was, after all, thirty-two. But we were supplementing her income from time to time.

What if we had pulled any financial support unless she stopped seeing M or unless she went to meetings daily or unless who knows what? Could we have checked on all of that? Would it have made any difference?

Looking back on that summer, I think I was so overwhelmed with anxiety, worry, and sadness that I was afraid to do anything that might rock Giana's boat. Giana had her dream job. She was working in an acute care vet hospital, assisting in a variety of departments, including emergencies and surgeries. I wanted so much for her to continue to find satisfaction and pride in the work she was doing. Wanting to believe that she was putting the Nubain and weed behind her, I didn't want to do anything that would create stress. Or was it my own distress I was calming?

While I didn't take many summer vacations because of work, that summer I went to the beach for a few days because Giana's father had rented a house, and some of the kids and grandkids were down there visiting. I reserved a hotel room for myself. Giana had managed to wrangle two days off from work, and I was waiting impatiently for her to arrive. I recall being on the beach, and she appeared over the dune in a pretty yellow-and-white sundress, her hair waving almost to her waist. I was so relieved to see her and have her nearby for a few days. She went swimming and surfing, but she was extremely quiet most of the time and was too thin. I alternated between worrying and telling myself not to worry. Wasn't she staying in the same house with her dad and siblings? It was a small house with little privacy. How could she be using?

One weekend a few weeks later, I was shopping not far from Giana's apartment and decided impulsively to drop in without calling. The bodybuilder ex-boyfriend, JM, the one who was initially responsible for the Nubain, who was no longer a boyfriend but a friend, answered the door. This was not good, I knew. He stood in the door and said that Giana and M had gone to get some coffee. Later I questioned her closely about what he was doing there, and she told me that he had been evicted from his place and was just staying a few days.

Why didn't I tell him to get out of the way? What if I had told him I wanted to see the dogs and forced him to let me in? Would I have seen evidence that she had relapsed?

A week or two later Giana's sweet rescued boxer, Maggie, became ill again. Giana had adopted Maggie when Abby died and often said that Maggie was her favorite dog ever. Maggie was twelve or thirteen and had been through many surgeries and treatments, including having a leg amputated. This was the end of the road. Maggie's death had been looming for a while, and Giana and I talked about it many times. She was worried that she was keeping Maggie alive for herself, not for Maggie. I told her over and over again that she had provided Maggie with several great years of care and love after the rescue. I reassured her that she would know when it was time. For a long while she convinced herself that Maggie still had, on balance, good quality of life, but with this new setback that balance tipped the other way. She called me abruptly one day at work and said she was going to put Maggie down and asked if I wanted to be there. I asked her whether she needed me to be there, and she said no, several of her friends at work would be with her. In one of her rehab journals, Giana wrote that she felt guilty about the last months of Maggie's life, because while Maggie had always been a loyal and loving companion, Giana felt she had neglected Maggie due to her addiction.

After Maggie's death, Giana's decline was swift.

~

For a while, my oldest friend and roommate, Dina, and I had been planning a trip to Europe for the fall of 2012. I had been reading widely about World War II for several years, and I wanted to tour some related sites. We planned to go first to Krakow, Poland, near Auschwitz, and then we were headed to Italy. Giana was to stay at my house with her remaining dog, Jade, a pit bull she had rescued about four years earlier as a puppy. We left on the morning of September 4. My friend James came by to wish us well, and he assured Giana that she should call him if she needed anything. I was uneasy; Giana seemed fragile and especially quiet. She claimed she had been going to meetings but was short on details.

Message from rehab: *They have to do it themselves. You can't do it for them. You have to live your life. You have to establish boundaries.* Translation: *Go on your vacation.*

Shortly before we left that day, Giana was curled up in her favorite corner of the sofa with Jade, a throw quilt pulled over them. I watched her head for the basement bathroom, her handbag in tow. That she was going to use went through my mind.

Dina and I drove to Newark Airport and left her car in the long-term parking lot. After checking our luggage and clearing security, we sat at a counter to have a snack. My phone rang. It was Giana. I remember looking at the phone and knowing immediately this wasn't going to be good news. Without any hesitation, she told me she had been fired from her job that morning for stealing medication. She told me she needed to go back into rehab. She didn't ask me for help; she didn't have to. She knew I would respond the way I did. There was no way I would have been able to relax and enjoy the trip. I retrieved my luggage, got the car, and drove home. Dina went on our vacation without me. I remember driving back to Philly, anxiously calling Giana every fifteen minutes to make sure she kept answering.

What if I had told her I couldn't help and had gotten on the plane?

I've thought a lot about this day since. Would the outcome have changed at all if I had told her that I was about to board the plane and she needed to call her father? Would establishing that boundary have had any effect? Addiction workers wedded to the AA philosophy are full of platitudes about establishing boundaries, but I haven't seen hard evidence of that working with opioid use disorder. What I have seen are grieving parents who regret having gone the tough love route, pushing away their children, instead of just embracing their children while they were still alive.

When I called Giana from the road, she said that she didn't want to go home until I was there. This made no sense, but I didn't question it. Nothing made sense. That evening she said she had pulled over into the parking lot of the gym to meet her dealer and buy Nubain. She had met him that afternoon because she was afraid of withdrawal symptoms before I took her to the rehab in the morning. I think it's difficult for nonaddicted people to understand how much avoiding dopesickness drives an addicted person's behavior—it wasn't about wanting to get high another night but about fear of the debilitating withdrawal symptoms.

That night Giana was very worried about getting arrested, not sure at that point if her employer would press charges. She and I and her father were hoping to salvage her career and hoped they would not, and in the end they didn't. I don't think the consequence of losing her job and imperiling her career, the loss of independence that it occasioned, and the crash of self-esteem that inevitably followed had hit home yet. She was more concerned about the animals she had left behind. In addition to her fear that she would get arrested, that's what she spoke about most that evening.

As with Keystone, she had called her insurance company and arranged for her admission to Valley Forge Medical Center, a private, for-profit hospital. I drove her there the next morning, September 5, 2012. I remember nothing of our ride there, but I do remember the long curving driveway, the old buildings with new additions, the lightly manicured meadow and gardens, the generally peaceful feeling of the place. I was relieved. I relaxed and let out the breath I had been holding since her phone call the day before. I waited in the lobby while she went through intake, made a bit uncomfortable by a large, scantily dressed man, asleep but very restless on a sofa nearby. At some point I went and asked the receptionist if he was okay—maybe someone should take a look. The receptionist assured me that he was just waiting for intake. He had come without an appointment. Eventually Giana came out to say goodbye and handed me her cell phone. The man was still moaning on the sofa.

What followed were several days of "blackout" while she was in detox, meaning we could not communicate. Since I was supposed to be out of the country on vacation, I decided not to go to work, at least not the first week. Almost no one knew I was at home in Philly, just my other kids, their father, and James. I found myself in an odd but comfortable bubble, free from incessant work demands, free from social interactions, relieved that Giana was safe and confined. I took long walks with her dog and tried to sort out my roiling head—how did we get here and where do we go from here?

What's all this?

In my ramblings, I discovered things about my neighborhood I'd never known: a straggly stand of lemon trees; the choking weeds, cracked asphalt playground, rusted chain-link fence, and deluge of litter around the nearby public school; the small mansion of a French settler whose surrounding land had been a large farm, some of which became the park the dog and I wandered through every day. I realize now that I still did not grasp the precipice we were teetering on: her possible death was not something I was thinking about. My basic optimism told me that, while this was serious, she could and would get well, she would be able to work, she would return, albeit battered, to the serious, organized, hardworking, ironic, and occasionally witty daughter with whom I shared a love of dogs and books.

Soon after Giana entered Valley Forge, I was looking for something in her car and came across a plastic bag with empty pharmaceutical bottles of Nubain in it. This indicated to me that the person who sold these to Giana was either getting them directly from the manufacturer or worked in a hospital and had access. I tucked them away, and I still have them, although I'm not sure why. That prompted me to look into her phone. Maybe I should have had qualms about her privacy, but I didn't. It felt as if her safety would be enhanced if I knew what was happening. I found many texts between her and her dealer, and I forwarded these to myself. On a visiting day I discussed this with her and told her I might want to show these to someone if she relapsed. I didn't realize at the time that threats like these have no weight against the pull of OUD.

Giana's intake assessment from Valley Forge lists her GAF score at 35. The Global Assessment of Functioning (GAF—out of use since the DSM V in May 2013) was a numeric scale (1 through 100) used by mental health clinicians and physicians to rate the social, occupational, and psychological functioning of adults. Here is the description of what a score of 31–40 means: ". . . major impairment in several areas, such as work or school, family relations, judgment, thinking, or mood (e.g. depressed adult avoids friends, neglects family, and is unable to work)." This seems accurate. In the intake interview, when they asked Giana what her strengths were, she replied that she was honest. This is the day after being fired from her job for stealing drugs and after lying all summer about going to meetings and being sober. So, illogical, impaired judgment, unable to work? Yes.

The notes are ambiguous about Giana's treatment for depression and anxiety. Her initial treatment plan, dated September 12, 2012, doesn't list anxiety and depression in the DSM IV diagnosis (this is a diagnostic tool that was discontinued with the publication of DSM V in May 2013). The initial physician assessment does list both as *symptoms*, a serious error. Major depressive disorder and generalized anxiety disorder should have been elements of her primary diagnosis, not symptoms of her addiction. Giana's mental health history preceded her substance use disorder by more than a decade. She entered Valley Forge under the care of a therapist and a psychiatrist and was medicated for these disorders. No attempt to contact her psychiatrist or her therapist is indicated in the notes. Strangely, depression and anxiety are listed under another category in the assessment called the "multidisciplinary problem list," and a check box indicates that they will be treated. Her primary diagnoses are listed as opiate dependency and anorexia.

Studies by medical professionals have noted that most rehabs are not treating both mental health and substance use disorders in an integrated, effective way. Often this is based on a belief that the addiction must be treated first, assuming that the person must stop the substance use before mental health treatment will be effective. There is also the confusion that can occur because depression and anxiety are common responses to prolonged addiction, and the thinking goes that you can't make an accurate diagnosis until the person is abstinent. In Giana's case, there was ample history of previous mental health diagnoses and treatment to conclude that these were not symptoms of her addiction but co-occurring disorders.

It is difficult to ascertain from the notes whether Giana was ever seen by a psychiatrist during her stay at Valley Forge. There is no note specifically indicating that she was. Some of the handwriting on the physician's order sheet is unintelligible, although there were orders signed by RNs, LPNs, a DO, and an MD. The DO was not a psychiatrist. I was unable to find information on the MD. Getting information about staffing at Valley Forge is difficult because their website has no staff listing, and it doesn't have a search function.

My son went with me twice to Valley Forge to visit Giana. We talked as we drove, and he mentioned that he felt the new boyfriend, M, was not the person Giana should be spending time with. Once again we were limited in what we could do because of Giana's age, but Greg felt that we should not allow him in any of our homes. Later M and Greg got in some heated arguments after it was discovered that M stole some alcohol that Lou had left in the house.

Greg's first impression of Valley Forge was markedly different from mine. He thought the buildings were shabby, and what I saw as the "lightly manicured" lawns, he saw as unkempt. He wanted so much to help Giana, but like all of us wasn't sure how. As her older brother, he felt a strong responsibility to help her get well but also, like the rest of us, felt confused about how to do that. Having once, decades earlier, had a teenage alcohol and cocaine problem that was resolved after therapy, rehab, and meetings, he committed to attending meetings with her when she was discharged. What he discovered along with the rest of the family was that OUD is not the same as alcohol or cocaine dependency. Its sudden lethality distinguishes it and requires a more urgent response.

Together at Valley Forge we attended "family education sessions," which were required if you wanted to spend the entire visiting time with your loved one. I would characterize these sessions as "scared straight" lectures in which the "educator" essentially harangued the group about the dangers of relapse, using details of his own relapses and the difficulties they caused other people. He was loud and at times funny, but I'm not sure this hour provided me with any insight whatsoever about how to help my daughter. My son kept giving me sideways looks that asked, what in the world is this about? I discovered that this staff member, who used the title "social worker," was part of the social work staff but did not have a social work degree.

I attended these sessions weekly when I visited. Once the session was given by another staff member, a female who was far less entertaining and much more formal. Like everything at Valley Forge, her dry talk was accompanied by many handouts. Giana would sit in these sessions impassive, with her required two-pocket folder on her lap, pen ready, occasionally making notes.

According to the records, Giana attended six 45-minute individual sessions with a master's-level staff person during her thirty-day stay at Valley Forge. Evidently, referencing the treatment plan, the two weekly sessions recommended for treating anxiety, the two for depression, and the two for addiction were the same sessions. If the notes are any indication, Giana received insightful treatment from this therapist at Valley Forge. According to the notes, at times this treatment did begin to address the relatedness of her mental health problems and her addiction; also the therapist wove in discussion of her "relationship addiction" and her history of eating disorders. The problem is that, according to the notes, she saw this therapist only six times in a month, with the last session devoted totally to "discharge planning." While a month of residential care composed of detox, education sessions, and group addiction counseling is insufficient for dealing with opioid addiction, depression, anxiety, and an eating disorder, the efficacy could have been maximized by coordination with her psychiatrist and therapist, and far more time in individual therapy.

The ninety-minute addiction counseling sessions Giana attended were held five times a week and led by a revolving group of staff, occasionally including her master's-level therapist but also by at least three others who were addiction counselors, one of whom was an intern. In Pennsylvania, there is a broad range of qualifications for the position of addiction counselor employed in a drug and alcohol treatment facility—anywhere from a physician to certification by a "statewide certification body which is a member of a national certification body or certification by another state government's substance abuse counseling certification board" (PA Code 704.7 (b) (6))—with apparently no education credential beyond high school required. It appears that all of those providing addiction counseling in Giana's group at Valley Forge had at least a BA, but none were medical professionals, and only one, the therapist previously mentioned, had a master's degree. These sessions cannot be categorized as group therapy but rather as addiction counseling.

Was there an underlying method and sequence to these sessions? It's hard to see that from the notes. In addition to a revolving group of counselors, patients entered and exited from the group as they were admitted or discharged from the facility. It appears that a given counselor may have begun the group exploring a specific topic and then continued the conversation based on patient response to that particular topic. It also appears that when a counselor was scheduled to implement the group two times in a row, discussion points were intentionally carried over from one session to the next but not from one counselor to another. Among Giana's papers from Valley Forge, there are an astonishing number of articles, pamphlets, and exercises about relapse: what situations are high risk for relapse and how to avoid them, how to handle them if they can't be avoided, how to examine your behavior to recognize that a relapse is coming, and what to do if you come to that conclusion. Since the groups consisted of people with all forms of SUD, there was evidently no distinction made between relapsing on alcohol and relapsing on opioids. Thus what was not discussed is the most effective means of preventing relapse for a person with opioid use disorder: medication.

In addition to the two individual sessions and the five group sessions weekly, the treatment plan included 12-Step meetings five days a week, daily community meetings, and patient education, which produced quantities of paperwork of all kinds. Giana's records included various worksheets, six of which originated from the "Social Work Department" and are called "Resource Activity Evaluations." These referenced various topics such as "Boredom" or "Assertiveness" and prompted the patient to give a short answer to four reflective questions. Giana's Valley Forge materials also include many worksheets about medical conditions related to addiction (HIV, Hepatitis C) that correspond to a list titled "Nursing Education Record." Some of these are in the form of little tests, such as true/false lists or multiple-choice questions. There is another set of six with titles like "Motivation and Recovery" and "Balanced Living." Most of these exercises required the patient to answer questions after viewing a video, questions such as "What situations and people in the video did you relate to most?" or "In what ways is your life currently out of balance?"

Giana left behind dozens of folders from various facilities containing photocopied worksheets, in some cases the *same* worksheets from one facility to the next. Giana was great at worksheets, note keeping, and organization. If she had been assessed by her ability to complete these exercises thoroughly, she would have been judged as very compliant to treatment, a rock star. In fact, after about two weeks at Valley Forge, she was made a team leader (patients were organized into teams coded by color), and I remember sitting in a family education session with her where she had a folder with paperwork to document the attendance of her team. A staff member commented to me that she was doing really well.

> *What if I had recognized early in her life that Giana was* too *organized,* too *tidy,* too *compliant?*

Giana had always been highly organized and compliant—in school, at home, in sports—in every way. My other children were messy, loud, forgetful, occasionally defiant, sometimes given school detention and even suspended. Giana never got in trouble in school. She never lost anything. She never spoke back to a coach or a teacher. Giana's clothing was organized by style and then color: athletic socks rolled neatly in one line, school socks organized by length and color in another. Every night her school bag and swim bag, clean and orderly, were placed by the front door, ready for the next day. But just below the surface, anxiety was raging, her orderliness and compliance a strategy to keep it in check. When that didn't work, her coping mechanisms extended to self-destructive behaviors like restricting her eating.

Giana recognized this pattern. In her journal written during treatment for her eating disorder, she wrote: "I think I have a need for planning and being organized, and I see that a lot here. It's like I throw myself into being so neat and organized to distract me. Sometimes it seems like a waste of time or stupid that I'm so organized about my menu, but I think it's what we need to distract us and keep us busy. And that makes me happy and comforts me. What is that?"

Giana's Valley Forge intake paperwork notes her eating disorder, and the treatment plan dated September 12, 2012, states that this will be monitored (not treated) by weight checks and patient education twice a week. The physician assessment describes her as thin and gaunt, and the nursing assessment lists her weight as 124 and her BMI as 19, the lowest within normal range for a 5'9" woman. She was slipping back into anorexia. Yet, for some reason, the staff at Valley Forge agreed on September 16 to grant her request for a low-fat diet and changed her sleep medication from Remeron (mirtazapine), which had been started on September 8, to Thorazine on September 18 because she complained that the Remeron was activating her appetite. There is little evidence of "patient education" about anorexia or eating disorders.

Unlike at Keystone, I don't recall ever being in a family session at Valley Forge, apart from the group education sessions described earlier that family members were required to attend in order to see their loved one. I was not asked to participate in discharge planning; Giana was discharged with a plan to go to an intensive outpatient program (IOP) called Rehab After Work, a chain of outpatient treatment centers located in Pennsylvania and New Jersey, and to attend the ubiquitous ninety meetings in ninety days. I don't know if Giana was ever contacted by anyone at Valley Forge after her discharge. A follow-up plan is not indicated anywhere in the records. If they had, they would have known that Giana stopped attending IOP prior to completion.

Giana as Color Day captain,
high school senior year, 1998

Chapter Nine

I picked Giana up from Valley Forge on a beautiful fall day. Jade had come with me and jumped wildly from back to front seat when she caught sight of Giana. I drove Giana directly to an NA meeting, which she left with a list of names and phone numbers—people to call if she felt troubled or at risk of relapse.

A week or two earlier, Giana had been encouraged to begin planning for her discharge. It wasn't really necessary to encourage Giana to plan; she was a natural at it. In a notebook she kept while at Valley Forge, she was making to-do lists starting a week after she was admitted.

- Check insurance
- Call PA Dept. of Education re: student loans
- Make appointment with PCP re: pap smear

Lists of things she needed: razors and tissues. Thank you notes she needed to write. And so forth. Celeste gave Giana a new planner as a discharge gift, which Giana began filling with tasks the day of her discharge. It shows the time and place of a daily NA/AA meeting, times and days scheduled for IOP, and therapy appointments twice weekly. She lists meals and outings with family members, walking in the park, playing with her nephews, going to the movies with me. She lists tasks such as getting her car serviced, going to the dentist, filling prescriptions. She was doing what she had been encouraged to do at rehab: take care of yourself, follow recovery recommendations, avoid idle time, but don't take on anything stressful. And don't be bored.

The advice was that Giana shouldn't rush back to full-time work, or work in a stressful environment, or work handling large amounts of money (like a cash drawer), and certainly not work in a vet practice or hospital, where there were drugs. What did that leave? Pet walking? No, couldn't take the chance of her being given the keys to someone's house and thus the contents of their medicine cabinet. Tutoring? Yes, she could tutor, but again, not in someone's house. We couldn't figure out what she was going to do all day to avoid being idle or bored. An hour for a meeting. An hour, two maybe, to walk and play with the dog. An hour of housework? An hour at the gym? Yoga? Volunteer work? I couldn't understand the contradictions: idle time is a trigger, stress is a trigger, boredom is a trigger, too much work is a trigger. . . .

I was very puzzled by the repeated discussion of boredom as a relapse trigger in rehab, although cycling through rehabs could in and of itself become boring, since the basic approach is similar from place to place, materials you've encountered before are handed out again, and the "program" is the same, even if it hasn't worked for you in the past. But Giana, bored? I didn't get that. As a teen and an adult, she always threw herself into her interests and worked with intensity—swimming, school, jobs, reading. She was always reading—Giana, her sisters, her father, and I passed books around even when she was a few months from death. And she was a curious child. She was my little travel buddy in Europe; when she was twelve or thirteen, we wandered in a circle around London, exploring the Roman ruins in Bath, punting on the Thames in Cambridge, visiting stone circles. In Greece I walked with her to the Parthenon on a very hot day, while her sister declined and stayed in the hotel room reading! We spent several days, definitely not bored, at Pompeii. I recall Giana schooling Celeste on Giotto's fresco cycles in the Scrovegni chapel in Padua. Bored?

And yet, as Giana's drug use escalated, her world narrowed. It was most evident in her loss of friendships, her increasing inability to get along with people, compounded by shame. Thus, she lacked the stimulus that is a natural product of interacting with others. Slowly, her adventurous nature evaporated. She was unable to travel. Once, in her twenties, she had flown to Colorado to surprise Louisa on her birthday, walking into a restaurant unexpected where Louisa's friends were celebrating with her. This type of spontaneity became impossible. If drugs displace everything else, perhaps adjusting to life without them feels like boredom.

~

After the loss of her job and her discharge from Valley Forge, Giana gave up her apartment. She planned to live in the vacant house that had been our family home, then her father's home. He had moved, and the house was going to be sold eventually. Sometimes the plan was for her to live there, with me staying there temporarily; sometimes the plan was for her to live there with M. It was all very vague, as were the whereabouts of M. Sometimes he was around, sometimes not. Everything was vague, because how could anything be concrete with two very ill and unpredictable people who were hanging on by a string?

One thing we undertook to keep her busy was thorough housecleaning and clearing out of stuff that nobody was ever going to use again in the family home. We packed bags for delivery to the Salvation Army, put out boxes and boxes of trash, and went through closets that hadn't been disturbed in a long while. Giana and M painted a few rooms; Giana and I bought some new curtains.

Giana went back to waitressing part time at the restaurant where she had worked before and during vet school. I also had her doing volunteer work, mostly data entry and filing, where I worked. It gave me some reassurance to have her in a cubicle near my desk, busy and productive. She was very efficient, as she had always been. She usually came in the afternoon and left after a few hours to go to IOP. M was supposed to be in an employment training program near the Rehab After Work that she was attending. Sometimes she would leave my office early, saying that she was meeting him for coffee after his program ended and before hers started. I always wondered if she was really going to IOP, if she was really meeting M for coffee. I had the urge to stealthily follow her, or even hire a private detective to follow her. Then my more practical self would say, *Stop being ridiculous*. Turns out I should have followed my gut. On an intake form at a later rehab stay, she wrote that she had stopped attending Rehab After Work prior to completion.

That fall I bought a Crock-Pot. I had never used one previously, and in recent years with no dependents at home, I usually fixed a quick salad or heated up some soup when I got home from work. But I began to cook in the Crock-Pot almost daily so that Giana and M could come over for dinner—a way of getting to see her even more often. If I made too much, I gave meals to my son and his family. Having the smell of food in the house and a hot meal always available was suddenly comforting.

True to his word, sometimes my son accompanied Giana to meetings. They frequently attended one near my house where they both felt comfortable. Sometimes they came to dinner before or after the meeting. Giana took the beginning steps of engaging a sponsor, and calls and sessions with her sponsor started cropping up in her planner. Ninety meetings in ninety days. This was the second time she had been given that prescription. What I should have thought was this: when I had been given an antibiotic that didn't cure the urinary tract infection, I was given a different antibiotic. When Giana was given an asthma medication that didn't stop her wheezing, they gave her a different one. When my mother was given a medication that lowered her blood pressure but made her cough, they switched it. If something doesn't work, why do it all over again the same way? But in the case of addiction, the fault is generally ascribed to the patient, not to the prescription.

In her journal Giana wrote: "Almost every day I have looked back to the very small amount of clean time I had at Keystone and afterward and wished so badly that I could have it back and that I had held on to it. I probably think about it every day, several times a day and wish I could just go back to that. Why did I throw it all away? Why did I do this to myself again?! And the self-loathing just starts. . . ."

Climate change may explain why my memories of Halloween three and four decades ago involve how to dress kids warmly enough and still have the costume be visible. My recent Halloween outings with your nieces and nephews have been in milder weather. Do you remember me trying to get costumes on over the puffer jacket? Do you remember shuffling through fragrant piles of leaves that ignited your allergies on the street near our house where a few neighbors had built elaborate scary displays, witches dancing around a cauldron (usually filled with spiced cider that they offered everyone), or coffins with shrouded figures rising out of dry ice?

I was not one for store-bought costumes and not much for masks. I remember making bug costumes out of two pieces of thick cardboard, joined at the shoulder with string, to be worn like a signboard advertisement. We painted them ourselves. You were once a ladybug. In addition to the cardboard front and back, we took a headband and created antennae from pipe cleaners. A few spots on your face painted with makeup, and voilà!

I have a picture of you in my arms, dressed in a homemade ghost costume made from a sheet. You were probably two, turning three in January. A piece of the costume is wrapped around your lower face, so just your serious dark eyes are peeking out. The look in your eyes says, *why are we doing this?*

Another picture, a few years later, of you in a shiny yellow-gold nightgown, a tiara on your head, shimmery makeup and sparkly shoes. Princess time.

While I was good with the costumes, I wasn't so great at the decorating. We always managed to carve a pumpkin, and we taped all the school-made witches and bats and spiders on the windows. That was about it. But that's why we had to go to Grandmom's! I have a picture of you and Louisa on her porch, a huge pumpkin on the table, surrounded by seasonal gourds and displays of colored leaves. Then coming up her steps were smaller pumpkins, all carved differently: scary faces, happy faces, silly faces. Do you remember that she used to put orange votive candles in paper bags and weight them down with sand, marking a walkway to her door for the trick-or-treaters? Did they get candy? No, from her they got homemade iced cookies in Halloween shapes, packed in little baggies. We often made them with her, a tradition I'm still carrying on with your nephews and nieces.

And that's why I was so happy when you came into the kitchen in the fall of 2012, a few weeks after your release from Valley Forge, and when you saw that I was making Halloween cookies with James's daughter, Jamie, you asked if you could help! You asked if you could make a batch to take to a costume party given by someone you had met at an NA meeting. *A good sign!* I thought. Making friends and socializing with sober people. We had fun devising a witch costume—I just happened to have a very wonderful witch's hat in the basement.

~

Halloween came and went, and the entries in the planner continued, until suddenly, the week after Thanksgiving, they stopped.

Carving pumpkins with Giana's maternal grandmother, circa 1987

Chapter Ten

A week or two before Christmas, Giana brought M to my house for dinner and to decorate the Christmas tree. James and his daughter were there also, and I made dinner. The tree was very large, and I had already draped it with five hundred white lights. In the candlelight, Giana showed M various ornaments, and we laughed about how she and her siblings used to tease each other about which was the ugliest of the long-saved handmade ones. She looked well, seemed well, and I was happy.

She had started using heroin a few weeks earlier, but I didn't know it. I have wondered so many times since about how she felt carrying such a big secret and seeming so normal. Was she deliberately acting, or at that moment, that evening, did she actually feel well and normal? I've also wondered so many times about that relapse. Things seemed to be progressing, if her activities and her planner were any indication. I've speculated that M might have been in a different stage of the sober/relapse cycle than Giana was and that she couldn't keep herself sober while he was using. I found a sheet of paper in his handwriting giving Giana explicit directions for where to go to buy heroin. I don't know when that was written, but even in 2012 and 2013, opioid prescriptions were becoming harder to get. One pill on the street cost about thirty dollars. Nubain was expensive also. Once she decided to use, the turn to heroin, so common, might at first have been an economic decision, at eight to ten dollars a bag.

On Christmas Eve, Giana went to the traditional seven fishes dinner that her father and Uncle D always made. Some of her siblings and nephews were there, along with a few other guests. She was going to come back to my house afterward, as M was spending the holiday with his parents. In the morning, relatives and children and grandchildren would come in their pajamas to my house, always decorated with fresh greens and many candles, and as usual, we would open the bounteous stockings I always stuffed, eat brunch, and then open gifts. My Christmas Eve plans were to go to an open house at a friend's with James. After Giana left for her dad's, I went into the guest room where I had been wrapping gifts earlier, to get a gift bag, and saw her silver makeup case on the dresser. I wasn't looking for it, but when I saw it, I immediately opened it. The surge of adrenaline that followed made me dizzy and dry mouthed. In the case were syringes, a spoon, and packets of white powder. I knew what I was looking at.

I thought about what to do. Get in the car and drive to Lou's Christmas Eve dinner to confront her? Take the case and confront her when she got home? I tried to imagine how that would play out and stupidly couldn't get past how it would destroy the next morning's festivities for the grandchildren. Obviously I was still in denial about the danger Giana was in. I went to the party confused, ate nothing, socialized distractedly, and talked to James about what he thought I should do. I decided I had to tell Lou and that we needed to confront her together.

In the morning I called Lou, told him what was happening, and asked if he could come in the early afternoon. He was speechless—then. It was a strange Christmas morning, the ritual unfolding as usual, but with me going through the motions robotically. My son was just leaving and getting his kids in the car as Lou arrived. I remember that when Lou walked into the house, Giana looked up and said, "Dad's here?"

His anger, which had been percolating over the past few hours, rose like a geyser. "So now it's heroin?" he shouted. I instantly realized that he and I had not adequately prepared for what we were going to say and what we were going to demand. He continued to holler, "Do you want me to buy it for you? Because eventually you'll have to be a prostitute!"

At the time, I thought of this as simply rage and despair, and he would not have known where to buy heroin anyway. His fear was that she would become a prostitute or a criminal. Interestingly, heroin is medically prescribed in some European countries as an alternative for patients who have not responded to other forms of treatment, both to keep them from becoming criminals and to protect their health. Properly dosed, medically supervised, free from unknown and deadly additives like fentanyl, this is a way to keep people alive as medical professionals continue to try various methods to get them into remission.

Giana's reaction to our confrontation was unlike anything that had happened up to this point. Prior to this, when she had reached a crisis point, like getting fired, she was remorseful, sad, seeking help. She had checked herself in to rehab twice. Now she was angry and resentful. What was happening? I can only imagine that she was still in the honeymoon stage with heroin and was not interested yet in giving it up.

Lou was so angry that he didn't stay long, and we had gotten nowhere about what to do next. I suggested rehab, and Giana said no. After Lou left, Giana said that she just wanted to go back to the house and be alone. I was surprised she thought I was just going to let that happen—did she really think I was that dense, or was she desperate? I knew what it really meant and said no. I told her that she couldn't stay there, at least for a while. She said she needed to go get some things, and I insisted that I would go with her. When we got there, I went up into her room with her, overseeing everything she was packing. Hostile, she told me to go downstairs, and I said no. She threw some packets of heroin on the floor and yelled at me. I wouldn't leave her alone. Eventually she packed some clothes, and we went back to my house. She went to bed and didn't speak to me.

Merry Christmas.

I remember the next day well, because I was having some windows installed. Giana moved from bedroom to bedroom as the installers worked, sick from withdrawal. At one point, I was passing through the upstairs hallway and glanced into the guest room. She had gotten out of bed and was changing her clothes. The door was half open. She was naked, bent over, pulling off her socks. Her skin had a bluish hue, and she was very thin. She startled when she saw me and straightened up. On her side was a new tattoo, one I hadn't seen before. It was script in a fancy font. My first response was anger, thinking that she had frittered away money on nonsense. I closed the door and hurried away, not knowing exactly where the window installers were in the house.

Later I wanted to know what the tattoo said. The quote was from a song called "If You Don't, Don't" by a band called Jimmy Eat World, which of course I had never heard of. The lyric was: "Even if your heart would listen, I doubt I could explain." A part of me responded by thinking, *What a self-indulgent, adolescent bunch of BS.* But not all of me—the words were sad. Giana was sad, isolated. *Even* if your heart would listen—implying that no one would—I *doubt* I could explain—meaning that she herself did not understand what was happening to her. The words expressed how she saw herself and her inability to connect and communicate.

That lyric also represents the way I have felt since the first day I found out about her drug use. The stigma was so great—more then than now, I think, although maybe I just don't care about it anymore. Then I couldn't imagine talking about it with any but my closest friends and family. I couldn't conceive of having to field the questions, or worse, endure the silence. I had no idea how to understand it myself, so how could I explain? Yet even now, as I bare my soul about it, I don't know if I can explain. The complexity of the problem—opioid addiction's intractable nature; the compounding brought on by severe depression and anxiety; the substandard treatment; the lack of the very resources, such as MAT, that might have made a difference; the guilt at having failed to help her; the dismay about what her loss means to my other children; the grief and sorrow that is every day like a knife in the heart—how can one actually explain?

My reaction to the tattoo was familiar—she would anger me, but then something she said would tear me apart and drive home to me her despair. My anger would vanish, and I would be frantic trying to figure out how to restore her to being well.

Was it surprising that I was unfamiliar with the music, despite how close we were?

By and large, my musical growth, and to some degree my encounters with popular culture, ended about 1970. Who had time to listen to new music, watch new TV shows, go to the movies? There was barely time to sleep, given kids, housework, work, and school. Yes, I still read and went to art museums, but the other stuff went by the wayside. Apart from jazz, swing, classical, and opera, which seemed not to penetrate at all, my older kids listened to what we listened to—Dylan, Simon and Garfunkel, Springsteen. Celeste still occasionally reminds me that when she was twelve, I wouldn't allow her to go to a Rolling Stones concert. The Rolling Stones must have been past their prime at that point, but she still wanted to go, and it still ticks her off that I wouldn't let her! We had a record player—there were no "personal devices" then. Yes, they found popular music stations on the radio. I recall long car rides with one radio where everybody got a half hour. My half hour was silence. Somewhere in the late seventies, I think we started using cassette tapes as well as records, and in the eighties the older kids started getting music for birthdays and Christmas—Cyndi Lauper? Madonna? There was MTV, when I allowed it. Anyway, by the time Giana began listening to music, it was through headphones. When she was a teenager and zoning out to music at long swim meets, I think there was some rap. But I really don't know. She was buried in a swim parka with a Walkman. After college, her music tastes began to change to what I now recognize as "pop punk" or "alternative rock" or even what is called "emo." Emo originally meant "emotional hardcore punk rock," but it's often associated with confessional, introspective, emotional lyrics, often about romantic love. This fits with Giana's depression and her repeated involvement in painful relationships. Many of the CDs that I found among her things when she died were from the early 2000s. That her musical taste hadn't evolved reflects that she was stuck in an adolescent frame of mind long after she ceased to be one.

That afternoon, I moved around the house, cleaning furiously, in despair and angry that I had been left alone to deal with her. I was actually glad that she was sick; it made me sure that she didn't have a secret stash somewhere in my house. Late in the day, she asked if M could come over. She said he didn't know about the heroin. I hesitated and then did precisely the wrong thing. I said yes but that I needed the three of us to talk about this. She agreed but said she wanted to tell him first, alone. I so greatly underestimated her capacity to lie. And his.

What I didn't know then was that Giana and M had been using together since November. When he came that day, she talked to him first, alone, as I had agreed she could. I thought she was telling him what had happened; in reality, they were using and hatching plans to use with these new restrictions—that she was in my house, and she would only have whatever money she could make waitressing because I wouldn't be giving her any more money. Later that week, she did go to work a few days. But then something else happened; I never found out exactly what, but by New Year's Day, she told me the restaurant said they didn't need her at the moment because things were slow. I had suspicions at the time that this wasn't true—no real reason, just intuition. I was right. Later, I read in one of her notebooks that M had somehow gotten her fired, and she was angry, which accounted for M's absence for a week or two.

She continued to refuse to go back to rehab, and Lou thought we needed to try something else—Suboxone. A friend's son had been treated with it when he was addicted to pills. I had never heard of it before. Lou made an appointment with the therapist whom that young man had been seeing. Giana was still very angry and inaccessible, only agreeing to this because we insisted, and at this point she was totally dependent on us. I remember sitting in the therapist's office; he was a bear of a man with a cozy, messy office, lots of books, and stacks of paper. Giana was wearing a hoodie pulled so it shielded a lot of her face while we were trying to have a conversation. Lou asked her why she had started using heroin. She said sarcastically, "Because I wanted to get high." I wanted to slap her, but the therapist nodded his head with understanding. I think that was the only thing Giana said in the whole session. I asked him about NA meetings and the 12-Step protocol. He was noncommittal and said that if people felt it was helpful to them, then they should go, in addition to Suboxone and therapy. This therapist worked with doctors authorized to prescribe Suboxone, but Giana refused to see him again. She told us that she wanted to pick her own doctor, and within a week she found a psychiatrist who could prescribe Suboxone and provide therapy, so she only needed to see one person.

I insisted on knowing the name and address of the doctor and checked him out. He was legitimate and connected to a very good hospital (not a rehab facility). Once this was done, we allowed Giana to move back into the family house, with M there a lot of the time. He had done a masterful job of convincing me he was sober. When he was not around, I stayed there, or Giana stayed at my house. I arranged for her to do some volunteer tutoring with kids I knew needed it, in my presence. It wasn't that

I didn't trust her with kids; it was that I was worried she might fail to show up.

The last birthday we had together—Giana's last birthday, January 21, 2013—was not a good one. She had just begun staying again at the family house with M. I invited her to come to my house and asked what she wanted for dinner. I invited Lou and told Giana that M could come as well. She came without him, saying he was sick—we later found out he had relapsed on alcohol in addition to heroin. I had made some sort of pasta at Giana's request, likely with sausage. I probably got an ice cream cake, her favorite. We ate, Giana replied to Lou and me in monosyllables, if at all, and when dinner was finished, she went into the living room and turned on the television. She was inaccessible, remote, rude—and in withdrawal, although I didn't know it.

As it turned out, she visited the doctor she had chosen for the first time that day. I have his notes. Some of this first visit was a history, but it contains information I haven't encountered in other notes. For example, it states that Giana had used Percocet and OxyContin to "fill in," presumably when she had been unable to get Nubain. When I mentioned this to Louisa, she told me that she had seen some Percocet in Giana's room and asked her about it. Giana said that my mother had given it to her for her back. It was left over from before my stepfather died. *Hmm*, I thought. Could be true. He had many prescriptions for pain. And I had forgotten about the back injury Giana sustained at work when lifting a heavy sedated dog off a table, and the subsequent emergency room visit, orthopedic doctors, and the opioid prescriptions. What role had that played in everything? At that time, 80 percent of people who became addicted to heroin began with prescription drugs—and the percentage is still very high. Although she was definitely using Nubain when she had the back injury, the access to prescription opioids may have pushed her further along.

The psychiatrist's notes affirm that Giana began using heroin in November 2012 and used daily until January 1, 2013, confirming that M had come to our house with a supply the day after Christmas. The notes say that she was off for almost two weeks—the weeks she was mad at him about whatever happened at the restaurant, I presume, and when she had no money—and that she had begun using again a week earlier, about January 14. I assume when they reconciled, he came with some money.

When Giana saw the doctor on her birthday, she had been using four bags a day for the past week, but the past two days had gone without. On her birthday appointment, he writes that Giana was clearly in withdrawal, hence her behavior at dinner. The doctor prescribed Suboxone film, and Giana's depression medication was changed from Paxil to Cymbalta. She had a prescription for Xanax as well, from a previous doctor. The plan was to continue seeing this psychiatrist every two weeks, going to meetings (or claiming she was), and doing volunteer work. I'm not sure anything would have made a difference at that point, but I think we should have forced Giana to live with me, taken away the car, barred M from the house, increased the therapy to several times a week, and drug tested her randomly. One problem among many was that I didn't know anything about random home drug testing. No one at Keystone or Valley Forge ever brought it up. I had no idea at that point that one could buy a drug test for heroin in any pharmacy.

Of course, Giana had just turned thirty-three. If we had refused to let her stay in the family house and refused to subsidize the car, she might just have bolted to the street rather than stay with me without M and be drug tested. And what about all those hours when I was at work? I remember reading that Paul Newman hired a "minder" to be with his son at all times—and who besides someone like Paul Newman could afford that? His son still died.

I don't know what happened with M, but he ended up in

residential treatment just before Giana called me on March 7, as I was driving back from a conference at Penn State. He may have had a positive drug test when he visited his probation officer. This was a recurring pattern: Giana and M would end up being admitted to treatment at the same time. In retrospect I believe that she was unable to endure the loneliness of her addiction without him. On the phone, Giana told me that she had been manipulating the Suboxone, was using heroin, and needed treatment. Her hostility was gone; she wanted help.

~

One of the downsides of methadone, oral buprenorphine, and oral naltrexone is that they rely on the daily compliance of the patient, and people with SUD—like many people with various chronic and relapsing illnesses—are not always compliant. I remember watching a colleague struggle with her binge-eating disorder. She went up and down the scale, and with it her blood pressure and sugar levels fluctuated. She was on meds for both. Finally she gave up and had gastric band surgery. She lost a hundred pounds, her blood pressure and sugar levels returned to normal, and she was off the meds. A year later she had not returned to the doctor to have her band filled with the saline that constricted her stomach, and her weight was slowly rising again. Compliance is a tricky psychological requirement, especially when the desire to get high (or to overeat) is so very compelling. *Unable to change the behavior even when you are aware of and experiencing the negative consequences.* That is why the implantables and shots were developed.

I don't think Giana was ever committed to the Suboxone protocol; she simply went along with it to avoid a residential setting so she could continue to use heroin. As the psychiatrist noted, she was using heroin when she could get it, off and on for the four weeks prior to seeing him, at which point she was prescribed Suboxone. She was also seeing him only every other week, and there was no understanding or agreement with me or her father that we should oversee her ingestion of the film or that she should be randomly drug tested at home. Perhaps this setup works for some people, especially those who have been detoxed on buprenorphine, given Suboxone as part of inpatient rehab for a period of time before discharge, and then supervised by a doctor after discharge as part of MAT treatment. But for someone who had already relapsed twice after two inpatient stays—and given Giana's negative attitude after I discovered her heroin use—this was a recipe for failure.

Chapter Eleven

Imagine this!

Reader, imagine this. Imagine that your daughter has diabetes, as well as a diagnosis of depression and anxiety. Imagine that with this combination of illnesses, she is not always able to control her diet and exercise, and sometimes fails to take her meds or test her blood. Imagine that her blood sugar is high, and she goes to an emergency room, and they admit her. Imagine that while in the hospital, a stupid friend brings her favorite forbidden treats. She consumes them and her blood sugar spikes, and then imagine this: despite being sick and in danger, the hospital kicks her out, refusing to treat her because of her infraction. No other hospital agrees to admit her. She is given information about a safe house where other people with diabetes live together and try to control their diabetes by developing compliance through attendance at daily groups run by a counselor and by attending meetings with other diabetes patients. The counseling staff discourages medication. The house is run by a person who has heart disease and does well with consistently exercising and controlling her own diet, but has no medical training.

Unimaginable? Yes, if your daughter has diabetes. But not if she has an opioid use disorder.

This is what happened to my daughter at the Malvern Institute, which their website described as "one of Pennsylvania's most comprehensive and effective substance abuse treatment centers." Giana checked herself in to Malvern voluntarily on

March 7, 2013, sick and asking for help. Her insurance company, which referred her to Malvern, agreed to cover a month's stay, and I took care of the $670 co-pay. After five days in detox, conducted with buprenorphine, she was moved into a room with three young girls, all heroin addicts, all recently detoxed.

On March 11, Giana's counselor wrote: "Giana attended her first group today. She introduced herself and gave a brief addiction history. She appeared tearful while discussing her history of relapse, and told the group she is struggling to stay in treatment. She was receptive to their feedback."

On March 12, the same counselor wrote: "Giana attended group today. She told the group that she is really struggling with cravings and doesn't know how to overcome them. She was encouraged by the group for her honesty. She also told the group that she thinks she needs more treatment than thirty days, and wants to discuss PHP [partial hospitalization program] with residential with her mother during the family session." Giana had done this before when in treatment for anorexia. When the insurance company reduced their coverage from residential care to outpatient treatment, we had paid the difference to keep her in a residential setting.

On March 14, the same counselor wrote: "Giana attended group today, but participated only minimally, when prompted."

On March 15, the same counselor wrote: "Giana attended group today. She told the group that yesterday was a difficult day, that she really struggled with cravings and body aches, stating that she believes day 7 off Suboxone is always most difficult for her. She seems motivated for change." (Suboxone was used for Giana's detox at Malvern but discontinued as she moved to the treatment phase. What is now commonly recommended, although not often done, is to continue the buprenorphine in a reduced dose to stave off cravings and remove that barrier to allow the patient to respond well to the other aspects of treatment.)

Apparently Giana was not "motivated for change." A few hours after the above note was written, Giana was being discharged for using while in treatment. The evening before, one of Giana's roommates had been able to sneak heroin into the facility and shared it all around. That girl was kicked out of the facility that night; another two were discharged in the morning. That day Giana admitted to her counselor that she had accepted the heroin and used. Giana was tested, and when the result was positive, she and her counselor called me and told me to come get her. I remember that call. Coincidentally, I was with my therapist when I saw Malvern's number come up on my phone. I picked up, and Giana and her counselor were on speaker. I remember saying to Giana something like, *I'm very disappointed about this, Giana.* And I remember her response, which was something like, *Not as much as I am, Mom.*

Unable to change the behavior even when you are aware of and experiencing the negative consequences.

While I was waiting in Malvern's lobby, I complained to the person I was dealing with that they were making her leave when she had been honest and badly needed residential treatment, and adding insult to injury, they had failed to control the environment. A male employee in the lobby interjected himself forcefully into the conversation, saying something like, *Seventy-eight people in here are following the rules. Four people didn't. Whose fault is that?* And, *We can't keep drugs out! How are we supposed to keep drugs out?*

At discharge Giana's GAF score was 46. Giana's diagnosis, in addition to opiate dependency, was listed as depression with anxiety. In two separate notes on her discharge paperwork, her prognosis was listed in one place as "guarded" and in another, "poor."

What kind of medical facility kicks a patient out under these circumstances?

In her book *Inside Rehab*, Anne Fletcher discusses this treatment issue. She quotes an article as early as 2005 in *Counselor* magazine by William White and colleagues that argues that expelling people for being symptomatic of the disease being treated is "illogical and unprecedented in the health care system. . . . For other chronic health care problems, symptom manifestation serves as a confirmation of diagnosis or feedback that alternative methods of treatment and alternative approaches to patient education and motivation are needed" (Fletcher 344–5). All of Malvern's indicators suggest that they saw Giana as a very sick young woman. Yet, when acting in a way that is common in a chronic relapsing disease, she was kicked out of the facility for that behavior without regard for whether she was medically safe.

Many studies by medical professionals have documented the deep difference between addiction treatment that is recommended by the medical community and most treatment that is available. The extensive 2012 study done by the National Center on Addiction and Substance Abuse at Columbia (CASA Columbia) noted: "Given the prevalence of risky substance use and addiction in America and the extensive evidence on how to identify and address them, continued failure to do so raises the question of whether the insufficient care that patients with addiction usually do receive constitutes *a form of medical malpractice* [emphasis mine]. It also signals widespread system failure in health care service delivery, financing, professional education, and quality assurance."

When Malvern refused to continue her inpatient treatment, we were unable to find a bed for Giana in another inpatient facility. (The discharge paperwork stated that she was being transferred to another facility, but that did not happen.) The evening of her discharge, she came home. It was a confusing night of fruitless phone calls to various residential facilities while she cuddled on the sofa with Jade. We didn't have a conversation about Giana staying at home. For me, I was convinced that if she couldn't be protected in a twenty-four-hour facility, I was even less likely to be able to safeguard her. I think she was afraid to be home as well. The next day we connected with a "recovery house" for women in Pottstown, Pennsylvania, recommended by Malvern. Malvern allowed Giana to be in their PHP–they had an arrangement with this recovery house by which they picked up patients daily for the five-hour program and returned them in a van.

I was dejected but determined to keep on trying. At this point, I surely should have begun to ask more questions, taken a step back and looked at this whole industry, and asked whether they really did know what they were doing. Giana was depressed, guilty, and ashamed.

The recovery row house was in a struggling neighborhood; a men's recovery house was a few doors down. No men were permitted in Giana's house, not even fathers. When we took her, Lou had to wait on the front porch. We had been told that she needed to bring her own food and bottled water, so we went shopping on the way. Although the population of the house kept changing as women relapsed, left, entered, or were sent by court order, there were six or eight women in the house at any given time, an interesting mix of older women with alcoholism and girls eighteen to twenty-five with OUD. Giana seemed to be the only one between thirty and forty-five. We paid weekly for Giana to stay there. She shared a room with another client and shared the only bathroom with all the residents. There were expectations such as daily attendance at an AA or NA meeting; often the residents walked together to one nearby, escorted either by the "house mother" or the lead resident, who earned that responsibility. The young lady who was in that position when Giana arrived relapsed a week later and was kicked out.

The recovery house had a curfew, and residents were not permitted to spend the night out unless they received a pass to visit family. Several of the residents were in PHP or IOP programs at Malvern with Giana; the others were expected to find jobs. The "house mother" was a recovering alcoholic with no formal medical or clinical training who oversaw this house and another one run by the same network. Giana liked her but detested living there. I couldn't blame her—the place was shabby, depressing, and crowded, especially the bathroom situation. She asked for books, and I brought her plenty. I think she spent a lot of time reading alone in her room, although she did learn to play several card games with some of the residents. One night when the house mother wasn't there, Giana had an asthma attack and was taken to the hospital by an older resident who had a car. The woman stayed with Giana for about five hours until the emergency department let her go. Giana was grateful, and they became friends; the woman taught her how to knit, which really surprised me. Giana had never been interested in anything domestic except that she liked to clean, and that was for reasons other than domesticity. But cooking or sewing—no. I used to knit and tried to teach my daughters. They were less than interested. Giana said the knitting was supposed to mimic repetitive coping behaviors—another relapse prevention strategy. She knit through NA meetings. I don't think she ever made anything except long panels. In her bedroom when she died, there was a green-and-yellow patterned panel, knitting needles still attached, a ball of yarn dangling.

At the time Giana was staying in this recovery house, there were no regulations in Pennsylvania governing recovery or sober living houses. In addition to concerns about whether the houses are operated in a way consistent with professionally recommended recovery systems, there are more basic concerns about health and safety, taxation, and compliance with regulations governing rental properties. In December 2017, the General Assembly passed and Pennsylvania Governor Wolf approved new legislation that directs the Department of Drug and Alcohol Programs to license or certify drug and alcohol recovery houses that receive referrals from state agencies or state-funded facilities or receive federal or state funding. This will take effect in June, 2020, seven years after the time Giana lived in a recovery house.

Many states are grappling with this problem as the epidemic grows, and some states have adopted voluntary certification programs. There is no doubt that quality varies, that some houses are well-run and help people stay the course, and that there are many caring and reputable people running these residences. It's also clear that some are no more than unregulated, poorly run boarding houses. If they are to become part of an effective and professionalized recovery system, regulation will be needed, including requirements for staff.

Another concern currently is the relationship of recovery houses to treatment facilities. An article in the *Philadelphia Inquirer* revealed that some treatment facilities pay "donations" to recovery houses that refer their residents to treatment ("Dumping Heroin Addicts in Philly" by Alfred Lubrano, November 13, 2016).

Shortly after Giana moved in, we had a conversation about her phone. The phone was always a problem. Phones are confiscated when patients enter residential rehab, and we had it disconnected, assuming she would be without it for at least a month. The phone had been returned when she was kicked out of Malvern. She begged me to reconnect it when she moved into the recovery house. There was a landline there, but use was limited and never private. Long-distance calls were not permitted, so she was unable to call Louisa in Colorado. She was spending most of the day at PHP and had no way to communicate with anyone from there, nor could I reach her when she was there. I was worried about her connecting with a dealer, but I decided to do it. I understood her sense of extreme isolation. I also wanted a way to text and call her as many times a day as I felt the need to, and was worried about instances just like the asthma attack that occurred a week or so later. But why didn't I reconnect the phone with the understanding that I could look at her texts whenever I wanted to?

A day or two after she moved, we pulled into a nearby outlet mall to go to the phone store, but at first she was unable to get out of the car. She was so depressed that she could barely speak or make eye contact. She sat curled in the passenger seat, staring at the floor. She had been going downhill since getting kicked out of Malvern. I tried one of my pep talks. Eventually she just opened the door and got out without speaking. Walking through the mall, we saw the children of a friend of mine shopping with their own children. Giana veered around a corner so they would not see us. As we huddled against a wall, her eyes welled, and she poured out to me her continuous, exhausting battle between wanting to get well and wanting to use, and her fear that she would never be well. I know from her writing that she felt an intense sense of shame about her situation. She also felt the aching loss of her career, her apartment, and her independence, "what my life has become," in her words.

After the phone store we went and bought sneakers. I recently discovered hers in a closet at Louisa's, barely worn. Louisa asked me to put them back where I found them.

~

Within a few days after Giana moved into the recovery house, she began the PHP at another Malvern Facility, Berwyn, from nine to two on weekdays. The Malvern website described Berwyn in this way:

Our Berwyn recovery center offers the following primary services:

- Drug & Alcohol Treatment
- Co-occurring Disorder Treatment

- Psychiatric Services (during PHP)
- Referrals & Collaborations with Outside Psychiatric Care (during IOP, GOP & individual)
- Addiction treatment at Berwyn focuses on the following areas:
- Codependence
- Meditation, Visualization, and Relaxation Techniques
- Relapse Prevention (including identification of key triggers)
- Cognitive Behavioral Therapy (CBT)
- Co-occurring Disorders
- Spirituality
- 12-Step Facilitation & Support
- Coping Strategies & Refusal Skills
- Recreational Therapy
- & More!

Our Berwyn drug and alcohol rehab is a one-of-a-kind recovery resource for residents of Chester County and the surrounding areas. It offers comprehensive addiction treatment at a variety of levels.

What more is there to say? Oh yeah, we haven't gotten around to mentioning our distinguished clinical staff yet!

~

Giana's PHP schedule was among the papers she left from Malvern. It was reminiscent of the schedules from residential programs, just less. . . . Instead of two community meetings a day, only one. No AA/NA meeting during program time—they expected you to do that in the evening. Each day was divided into seven time slots. The day began with a thirty-minute community meeting followed by a break and then a seventy-five-minute "small group," which was the addiction group counseling time, generally run by the same counselor. After lunch, a variety of sessions were scheduled, with titles such as Psycho-Ed, Multiple Family Group, meditation, yoga, and CBT. CBT was scheduled forty-five minutes once a week. These sessions were run by various staff members.

CBT is a proven treatment for many problems but is usually facilitated by a trained clinician to a stable group such as a family or a small group of patients, and usually for more than just the four sessions that PHP would allow. There is no mention of CBT in the progress notes, and since, according to the notes, participants in PHP came and left on an almost daily basis, it's unlikely that anything truly resembling CBT occurred. It's more likely these were one-off sessions using some CBT materials.

The first note from her new counselor in PHP, on March 18, states: "Discussed client struggling with depression and anxiety and how this impacts her recovery and point of view. Discussed client beginning *a gratitude list* to assist with negative thinking. . . . [emphasis mine]"

Negative thinking? Was her long-standing diagnosis of depression and anxiety the same as negative thinking?A gratitude list to deal with depression and anxiety? During PHP there were many references to exercises and activities like a gratitude list. For example, according to the notes, the patients developed "self-affirmations." Among Giana's papers from her time in PHP, there is a yellow piece of card stock titled "Self-Affirmations" in strong red and orange markers. Her affirmations include "I can be happy," "I can be successful," and "I have a college degree."

Also among her papers is a worksheet called the "Wise Voice Exercise," which was also used in another of Giana's rehab settings. According to the description of the group in which this was used, the patients were given direction in "identifying the wise voice" and "recognizing their inner critic giving negative feedback about their recovery and their self-esteem." Giana fills in a series of lines with adjectives: "I am not strong, smart, pretty, or thin enough." Her inner critic. Her wise voice changes the statements to, among others, "You are smart, kind, and compassionate."

There is also a worksheet where someone else in the group interviews Giana's addiction using questions printed on the worksheet. What does the addiction like best about Giana? *Weakness, never asks for help, has low self-esteem.* What does the addiction like least about Giana? *Her supportive family, and that she is intelligent and kind.*

According to the notes, the patients received education on topics including relapse prevention, coping skills, and conflict resolution and also practiced meditation, yoga, and played "Recovery Jeopardy." All of these topics and activities had become familiar with the exception of Recovery Jeopardy—that was a new one.

During PHP, Giana was pulled from activities in the afternoon or perhaps during lunch for individual sessions with her counselor. This occurred thirteen times between March 18 and April 18, or roughly three times a week, which included two family sessions with Giana, her father, and me.

I recall the counselor as an earnest young woman with an encouraging, professional demeanor. Giana liked her. She was a licensed social worker, which in Pennsylvania means that she would have a master's degree. (Those who have completed a post-master's clinical social work practice requirement are known as licensed *clinical* social workers, LCSWs.) Unfortunately, this counselor was unable to facilitate all the support for Giana that the Malvern website claimed would be available—including psychiatric services and/or collaboration with a psychiatrist. Contrary to the list of services from the website, there is no evidence in the notes that Giana was ever seen by a doctor, much less a psychiatrist, while in PHP, despite the claims that the program treats "co-occurring disorders" and provides psychiatric services.

On March 2, 2013, this counselor writes that Giana is having intense cravings and will have a phone conference with her psychiatrist the next day and discuss anti-craving medication. This is the psychiatrist whom Giana had been seeing before checking in to Malvern and had begun seeing again when she was kicked out of Malvern residential treatment. On April 3, the counselor writes: "Discussed phone conference she had with her psychiatrist who recommended Suboxone maintenance rather than naltrexone to address cravings. Discussed that counselor could discuss this with site director." On April 4 the counselor writes: "Met individually with client and site director to discuss client's ability to take Suboxone maintenance and attend PHP. . . . Staff expressed concerns with using Suboxone to address cravings and relapsing." In the end, Giana was not permitted to attend PHP if she followed the recommendation of her psychiatrist, despite the fact that buprenorphine was well researched by this time and recommended by many medical professionals as part of an effective treatment program. Malvern's decision does not seem to qualify as "collaboration" with a patient's psychiatrist, as promised on the website.

In the spring of 2013, I had a three-day meeting to attend in New York. As I often did when I traveled, I took my mother, who even in her seventies and eighties was up for adventures. We enjoyed traveling together on almost any type of trip. Years earlier, following a meeting in Salt Lake City, we spent a week touring the national parks in Utah with Louisa and one of her friends, where my mother, in her late seventies, went white water rafting. We took a two-week trip to Italy with one of my brothers to celebrate her eightieth birthday, where my mother walked miles every day. We went over rough roads in a truck to the Costa Rican rain forest and then the beach for Louisa's wedding. And we took many trips to San Francisco, Denver, Chicago, and New York tied to my work. In New York we usually added a day or two to my work commitment and tried to stay in different areas of Manhattan, depending on where I had to be. We almost always went to a play and several museums and took long walks. While I was working, my mother usually had a leisurely morning and then went out exploring on her own. On this particular trip, she wasn't feeling well. She was experiencing redness and pain in one eye, and she had been complaining of back pain and fatigue. I wasn't terribly worried about back pain and fatigue—she was eighty-eight! But this time she stayed in the hotel until I returned in the evening, and then we would go out to dinner. After the meetings concluded, we went to see a large exhibit at the Metropolitan, and she decided to do it in a wheelchair. Nonetheless, she tromped with me down to the 9/11 memorial site, at that time still under construction.

Thinking back on this trip, I remember that my primary concern about Giana was the depression. I felt very sure that she would not be able to stop using opioids unless her depression eased. I wonder now whether we should have explored a psychiatric hospital as opposed to rehabs, particularly if we had chosen one of the times when she had a few months sober under her belt but was still intensely depressed. I wonder about electroconvulsive therapy, which has made a comeback to treat some severe mental illnesses, including depression.

At the time of this New York trip, Giana was still living at the recovery house in Pottstown and attending PHP. My mother was aware of Giana's continuing struggles with depression, but she was not aware of the drug use. I saw no need to burden her with it, as there was little she could do. I knew if I told her, she would sit at home and stew about it. In the meantime, Giana, my mother, and I were planning a trip around the July Fourth holiday to visit Louisa in Colorado. I decided to take James's daughter as well. She had just turned nine and adored my mother, her own grandmother having died when she was only four. Neither Giana nor my mother had seen the house that Louisa and her husband had bought a few months earlier. I hoped that Giana would be in good shape and my mother would be relieved. It didn't turn out that way.

~

Giana completed PHP on April 19 and "stepped down" to IOP, which met three times a week, on April 22. At the conclusion of PHP, Giana had heeded the directive to find a job and began commuting into Philadelphia to work at a vet practice three or four times a week, a drive that took forty-five to sixty minutes, depending on the traffic. She planned her shifts at the vet practice around the IOP sessions. Since there was no way to get back and forth from Philadelphia to Pottstown and to accommodate both her work and IOP schedules, she had use of her car. In retrospect, this was a mistake, although the alternatives were difficult. She could have moved home at that point, taken public transportation to work, and not gone to IOP at Malvern. Maybe we could have found an IOP close to home, to which she could have taken public transportation on a schedule that didn't interfere with work. But the advice from Malvern and her psychiatrist was that she shouldn't move home yet.

Or perhaps she could have done volunteer work in Pottstown instead of going back to work. But her self-esteem was so low at that point, we thought that beginning to rebuild her career would be helpful, particularly if she was only working part time and didn't have access to drugs. At the new job, she would not. But without buprenorphine or even Vivitrol, she very likely was continuing to have strong cravings, and having her car provided her with more freedom to possibly use. In addition, her boyfriend was being released from his treatment program, and she wanted to resume their relationship, which no one—except for her—thought was a good idea. So many things to consider, with our input somewhat limited, given her age. Almost the only leverage we had was money. And our love. Over and over in the notes from every facility, she talks about how important it was to her that Lou and I still loved and supported her.

But everybody's nerves were frayed. Tensions about Giana caused arguments among all of us. Celeste was angry and for a while didn't want Giana or even me in her house. She felt as if our lives were being turned upside down, and she was especially concerned about the impact on her own kids. She was angry with me for not supporting her anger at Giana. It's very difficult to be patient with behaviors associated with addiction, especially after you've spent a lifetime supporting a sibling through various illnesses, including anorexia and deep depression. I've heard so many family members who have lost someone say something like, "I desperately miss the child, but I don't miss the addiction."

~

The notes from the IOP sessions at Malvern are extremely disturbing, not because they say anything disturbing about Giana but because they essentially say nothing about Giana. Her name is never used in a note and precise statements are repeated numerous times:

"Affect was appropriate, mood relaxed and upbeat." This was repeated verbatim on April 30 and May 2, 9, 13, 14, 20, 21, and 23. This is highly unlikely. Giana was struggling with cravings and was depressed and unhappy at the recovery house. And even at her best, Giana was not a person one would describe as upbeat eight times in three weeks.

"Pt was appropriately dressed, had an overall neat and clean appearance." April 30, May 2, 14, and 20.

"Pt and counselor worked on developing a therapeutic rapport and alliance during the session." Repeat of April 30, May 9, 13, 21, and 23.

Some notes appear to be about someone else:

On May 2 the counselor wrote, "Pt. was obviously upset when he discussed abuse that both he and his sister endured." This is repeated verbatim on May 14, 20, and 21. Clearly these notes are not about Giana. First, of course, the gender is wrong, but also, there is no history of abuse. Questions about abuse are standard at intake, and Giana always answered in the negative. Abuse never comes up in any other treatment notes from any facility or doctor.

One could easily come to the conclusion that all these notes are a cut and paste job, and sometimes (or always?) a cut and paste from another person's records. There is nothing in any of these notes that I can identify as particular to Giana.

There is a person named David Jones, DO, listed at the top of each note as "the provider." I doubt if Dr. Jones the provider ever looked at these notes. Surely he would have recognized the problems if he had. It would be worse to think that he did review them and did not see a problem.

The last drug test done by Malvern appears to be on May 9, which was negative.

The IOP note of May 30 indicates that Giana would be stepping down to a general outpatient program (GOP) "next week." GOP was scheduled for one evening a week with the same counselor she had in IOP. By the end of May, she was working more hours and was staying at home when she had an early morning shift. She had been seeing her psychiatrist once a week. He wanted to put her on naltrexone, but the recovery house would not allow it. So for that reason, and because she had been offered more hours at work, Giana moved home, and on June 17 she began taking naltrexone—or so I thought. That was the day she got the prescription. I was to watch her take it daily, given her previous noncompliance with Suboxone and her relapse history. Her hours at work increased to almost full time. I should never have agreed to oral naltrexone—I should have insisted on Vivitrol. But I didn't know any better.

Those weeks in June were characterized by hope, uncertainty, and panic. I woke up one morning about four and realized that Giana was not in the house. I looked around frantically for my phone and couldn't find it. Not for the first time, I had left it in my car. I live on an urban street where no one has a driveway or a garage. My car was parked down the street, but still I went racing out in my nightgown. There was a message from Giana, saying she had decided to stay at M's parents' house. I didn't necessarily believe that, but at least she had communicated. At least when she sent that message she wasn't overdosing or committing suicide, which I had begun to fear in my worst moments.

It all began to fall apart very quickly. Familiar and unwelcome behavior was kicking in—she was oversleeping, evasive about attending meetings, developing skin rashes, eating candy but not much real food—all signs that she was using. M continued to be around sporadically. I was told he was not using and was working, but who knew? I thought again about hiring a private detective to follow her. One day when she said she was going to a meeting at a very familiar church, I looked it up online and didn't see any notice about meetings there. I got in my car and hurried there, about a twenty-minute drive. I didn't see any sign of a meeting. When I got home she was sitting on the back porch. I confronted her. She told me I must have been at the wrong place, because she had been to a meeting. I had finally bought a home drug-testing kit, and I told her that I was going to test her, right then. She told me that the naltrexone would mess up the test, which wasn't true, but I didn't know that. I didn't believe her and took away the car again. After that she took public transportation to work, and I often picked her up if she worked until the end of the evening, about ten o'clock.

That spring at work, we were trying to plan camps with the housing authority in addition to the camps we ran in schools and community buildings, and it seemed that every detail involved extended negotiations. Some of these issues arose because we were working with people who had little experience running youth programs and weren't familiar with all the laws and regulations. Yes, we would love to hire some housing authority residents, but they must have these credentials as well as have criminal and child abuse clearances. No, even though this is a very nice basement, we can't put kids in here if there is no direct exit to the street. One day, only a few days before we were to leave for Colorado, I was in such a meeting and put my phone on Do Not Disturb. Thus, I missed a call from Giana that she had been in a car accident—in someone else's car. She had borrowed a car from someone at work. She called her brother and he went and rescued her.

Giana told me that she had borrowed the car and gone to buy Suboxone because the naltrexone didn't calm her cravings. I knew this was possible, as naltrexone doesn't work the same way as buprenorphine, and because by this time I had read about Suboxone being diverted and sold to addicts who were trying to escape dopesickness. But I didn't believe her. On an impulse I went and looked at the naltrexone bottle. The pills that were described on the bottle, the shape and color, were not the pills that Giana had been taking. Confronted with this, she told the truth. She had dumped the naltrexone and replaced it with an over-the-counter diuretic. She had borrowed the car to buy drugs; she was using and had been since the end of IOP at

Malvern. *Unable to change the behavior even when you are aware of and experiencing the negative consequences.* I told M to get out and not come back and told Giana that she was coming to Colorado regardless of how she felt. And when we got to Colorado, she felt terrible.

Giana with her paternal grandfather at a family event, circa 2004

Chapter Twelve

Giana, do you remember pushing Grandmom through the airport as we left on that trip? It was July 9. You were sick, and she was weak. We agreed that a wheelchair might be best for her and best for us, as we could speed through the airport, and it would allow us to board early. I was shepherding Jamie through the security line, where taking off her shoes and going through the metal detector wasn't a nuisance but an experience. It was her first time flying, and she was excited and oblivious to your discomfort.

Do you remember how unusually hot it was when we arrived that afternoon? Louisa took us down to the lakefront, where you and she dragged chairs to the water's edge and sat in the sun. In retrospect, that must have made you feel worse. Grandmom stretched out on a bench under a shady pavilion. When we returned to the house, both you and she went to bed.

Late in the week, when you began to emerge from your withdrawal cocoon, we drove up to Rocky Mountain National Park. You graciously went horseback riding with Jamie, although it must have been the last thing you wanted to do. Hunched in the saddle in your blue hoodie, you looked like every muscle and joint hurt.

Do you remember standing outside of Louisa's house talking about your future? You were finally walking around after a week of detoxing, and you asked me how you would ever be able to afford a house as nice as Louisa's. It was a crazy question at the time. I reminded you that you made more money than Louisa.

I noted that if you were single, you wouldn't need a house as big as Louisa's. You said, "Well, will you and Dad help me?"

I reminded you that we had helped all of you with everything we could: education, housing, travel, medical care, and on and on. And then I asked you, "Don't you know what's really preventing you from having all this?" And you replied that you knew it was your addiction. Still, I was so perplexed. How could you be thinking about what Louisa had and you did not when the only thing that mattered for you at that point was getting well? I guess it was an expression of loss at a time when you were not at all sure that you would ever get better.

At the end of the week, you were feeling better and were a bit more sociable. We went to a movie. You joined us for meals. But you were so sad. I had been telling my mother all week that you were sick, which was true in a way.

You didn't want to do what Dad and I suggested, a long-term residential placement, at least three months. And you didn't want to go to the facilities we wanted. But Louisa seemed to be able to talk with you. You and she sat at the kitchen table, looking through rehab options on her laptop. Finally, you agreed to enter Eagleville Hospital the day after we returned.

~

There are no general outpatient group notes in Giana's records from Malvern until June 27, almost a month after the note of May 30 that says that Giana would be stepping down "next week." The June 27 note says, "This was the first session of GOP for the group most members new [*sic*] one another from their time in IOP." There is a treatment note from July 2 that says that the group talked about recent relapses. Whether Giana shared about her relapse in this group is not mentioned, since Giana is not mentioned. It's not at all clear to me that she was even at this session. These are the only two GOP treatment notes in the records. There are no records of drug testing at Malvern during this period. Did she start GOP during the first week of June as the records indicated she would? Did she attend these two sessions? On her intake form at The Rose House, months later, she wrote that she had stopped attending GOP at Malvern. Whether she attended these two sessions, or an earlier one, the fact that the notes are in her file indicate that her insurance company was likely billed for GOP.

The discharge date from GOP is listed in the notes as July 16. By this time, Giana had been with me and her grandmother at Louisa's house in Colorado for almost a week. The day after, July 17, she entered residential treatment at Eagleville Hospital. The Malvern discharge paperwork indicates that she "completed treatment" despite her admission on The Rose House paperwork that she did not. There is no prognosis, but her GAF scored has elevated to 60. Somehow, according to Malvern staff, her GAF score rose from 46 when she was kicked out of Malvern residential for using to 60 when she had relapsed and was hospitalized elsewhere.

~

While Giana was in Eagleville, M was back at Keystone. The story I had been told—that M was working and not using—wasn't true. Giana was silently crying on the plane home from Colorado. She was frantic to get to our house, but we had to take my mother home first. I put it together later that he was being sent back to treatment, and she was trying to get home to see him before he went. She didn't get to see him before she herself went to Eagleville the next day, and in fact, she never saw him again. During this time, the two facilities permitted them to have one or two therapy sessions by phone. I don't know what was discussed in these sessions, but I do have a lot of correspondence between the two of them from this time. M's letters are long, passionate, and fevered. Everything he writes about is linked to how much he loves Giana, how much he wants them to be together forever, how her inaccessibility and indifference in the past has hurt him. He also writes about his commitment to recovery, although that is frequently framed by their relationship—he wants to get better because of her. Giana told me she felt that M was less "swallowed up" by his substance use than she was; that when she was actively using, she had little emotional capacity for anything else, and when she was not using, her battle with depression and anxiety drained her emotional resources. His sense that she was often just going through the motions was correct, although there were times when her attachment to him was strong. But her primary attachment was to heroin.

After Giana was safely at Eagleville, I took a day to unpack and prepare to go back to work. It was at this point that I realized some of my jewelry was missing. I didn't have a lot of very expensive jewelry, but I did have quite a bit that had sentimental value. Among the missing pieces were a small silver reindeer pin that my grandmother had worn every Christmas that I could remember, a silver bangle bracelet that Celeste had given me, a diamond and ruby gold ring that Lou had given me years earlier, a necklace that Louisa had designed and made for me, and most significantly, a fragile antique cameo brooch that had belonged to my great-grandmother and that my mother commissioned a jeweler to turn into a delicate gold necklace. I knew that Giana had taken these things and sold them for drugs and that it must have happened relatively recently. Later I realized that the money had also been used to fund M's needs, as he wasn't working and Giana was.

I was deeply hurt and angry.

When she called me the first time from Eagleville, I confronted her. She didn't deny it but said she didn't really know what she had taken; she had been in a fog. I told her to spend some time thinking about it and to make a list. I wanted to know where she had pawned them so I could try to at least get the cameo necklace back. She gave me the neighborhood but couldn't tell me any specific places. I found out later that this was because M did the pawning while she was working. I spent a blazing hot morning driving around visiting "cash for gold" places in the vicinity she had described. I encountered several extremely sympathetic storekeepers who knew exactly what was going on and felt very sorry for me. I never located the necklace.

When Giana reached Eagleville, she was already detoxed, having spent the past week at Louisa's house doing it the hard way. Eagleville was much like the other facilities where Giana had been treated except that there was at least one secure ward for psychiatric patients. The long list of interventions promised could have been cut and pasted from any of the rehabs she already attended. The diagnosis using the DSM IV was familiar: opiate dependence, anorexia, depression, episodic benzodiazepine dependence. They put her GAF score at 65, the highest ever. They listed her short-term goal as: "Giana will wants [*sic*] to develop coping skills to prevent relapse." Yes. Again.

The strategies to get Giana well and avoid relapse were also very familiar, the same topics, same handouts, same schedule: attend group therapy four times a week (which was really counseling, not therapy), attend relapse prevention two times a week, attend recovery seminars four times a week to learn more about the recovery process, attend life skills to learn how to live independently, and attend "an individual session once a week to deal with emotional issues and receive feedback." She will "identify seven triggers and identify one coping skill for each trigger," and she will "read a handout on coping skills and identify which coping skills appeal to [her]." I didn't have access to this at the time, of course, but at that point I was too angry to care what went on there. I wrote her a long letter, which Lou delivered the following weekend when he went to visit her and I did not.

After our trip to Colorado, I pressured my mother to get to the doctor. My mother was very casual about her medical care. Her "annual" checkup usually happened every two or three years. After the trip, I enlisted my siblings to insist that she go. We thought that perhaps her doctor could recommend some relief for the back pain—water aerobics? elder yoga?—or refer her to a specialist. However, she wanted to sort out her eye problem and prioritized that over an appointment with her family doctor. And it turned out there was an eye problem; a stitch from a previous cornea surgery had broken and was causing continual irritation. By the time she finally went to her family doctor, it was late July. Her checkup revealed nothing, and they ordered the usual blood panel.

As Giana's discharge from Eagleville approached, in early August 2013, Lou and I tried to persuade her insurance company that she needed additional time in a residential setting, but we were not successful. Her psychiatrist wrote a letter recommending a year of residential treatment. He and my therapist both explained that it could take eight months or more for Giana's brain to heal significantly. And despite the fact that she had been able to access heroin at Malvern, I felt the best chance of keeping her safe was in a monitored facility twenty-four hours a day.

After the insurance company said no to additional time at Eagleville, we tried to convince Giana that she should go to one of several rehab facilities we had found that, while not accepting insurance, had programs of longer duration. Caron Treatment Center was one of them, the closest one to us that would make it possible to visit often. We would pay. Giana refused. She decided to go to a recovery house in Levittown that she'd learned about at Eagleville. Later I found a reference to M having been discharged from Keystone to a recovery house in Levittown, so I assume she made this choice because of him. She was transported there by Eagleville.

Her phone was returned to her by Eagleville, and either Lou or I paid to have it reactivated; I don't recall this or the financial arrangements with the recovery house. Giana herself had no money whatsoever and no car. She still had health insurance because we were paying her COBRA. I spoke with her on the phone several times during the short time she was at the recovery house. She was to register at a mental health facility nearby after she arrived at the house—I assume for another outpatient treatment program. Having no car and no money, she was to take public transportation and then walk there, but she got lost, and when she finally got there just after two in the afternoon, they told her that intake was closed until the next day. She called me and said, "I can't do this." She sounded exhausted and defeated. I asked her if she would go to Caron. She said she would call me back, and did, a few hours later. She would go. I knew she needed further treatment, especially mental health treatment, and Caron's website and materials indicated that she would get it there. After a day of financial arrangements—we were pulling money out of our 401(k)s—and phone screening with Caron, Lou picked her up in Levittown and took her to Caron. I was taking my mother to get her blood work done and couldn't go. Lou said that she spent most of the time on the drive on the phone with M, explaining her decision and trying to calm him about it.

Giana and Elise at Caron Treatment Center, September, 2013

Chapter Thirteen

Lou and I went to see Giana the weekend after she entered Caron. Caron is a much larger facility than any Giana had been to previously; the primary Pennsylvania location where she was treated has close to three hundred beds. They have several residential facilities in Florida and outpatient services sprinkled along the East Coast. Giana was not yet permitted a pass, so we walked and talked and sat in the shade on the sprawling campus. We went to the small store on site that sells books, toiletries, and trinkets. Giana bought a green "I Hate Heroin" stretchy bracelet. I recall that during our visit we called Louisa, and the main topic of conversation was a memoir they were both reading, *The Glass Castle*, and whether Giana liked the food at Caron (code-speak for "Are you going to eat or will you lose weight?") Her siblings were as flummoxed as we about how to relate to her and what to say that might make a difference.

Located on the site of a former luxury hotel, Caron is nestled in a hilly rural area in central Pennsylvania. Very beautiful, very peaceful. I felt relieved by its inaccessibility and by the knowledge that the turnstile of admissions and discharges would be slower here, since most patients stayed for three months. At the time, all I cared about in an immediate sense was Giana's safety, and by that I meant no access to drugs and continual oversight. Of course, I had other hopes for the longer run, but her safety was paramount.

Her theft of my jewelry was still raw, but we'd talked and written to each other about it. Early in her Caron stay, she sent me this in a card, thanking me for continuing to support her. "I need to get better so that I can live a happy and productive life. I think that is the only real way I can say thank you. I know I have hurt you in many ways, and it may take you a long time to forgive me, if ever. All I can do is work hard, make changes, and eventually make amends—or at least try. I hope for now that is enough. I love you."

In truth, she was already forgiven.

Caron was founded as Chit-Chat Farm by Dick Caron, an alcoholic who embraced AA and believed that the 12 Steps and compassion could cure people who were seeking relief from their alcoholism. The Caron Foundation was incorporated in 1957. From the start, Caron embraced alcoholism as a disease, albeit a disease that must be cured by abstinence and adherence to the 12 Steps. A large sign when you pull into Caron's admission area announces its purpose and harks back to Caron's founding mission: "If you want to drink, that's your business. If you want to stop, that's our business." I winced when I first saw it, both because it seemed so . . . well, hokey, but also because by this time, I was not at all sure that alcoholism and OUD were the same disease, but rather cousins, like breast cancer and leukemia.

Caron is still steeped in AA philosophy and principles and integrates it into all aspects of its facility, even its landscape architecture. Near the admissions office there is a 12-Step walk, where one follows a path marked by each of the 12 Steps. The website states: "We combine evidence-based therapies with 12-Step principles that address all aspects of optimal wellness" and "Caron utilizes the 12 Steps as part of its integrated approach" (Caron website, August 2017).

Caron's endorsement of 12-Step principles was evident in

the treatment plans that resulted from assessments done during the first few days that Giana was at Caron. In her medical evaluation, done by a medical doctor, her diagnoses were:

Opiate Dependence, Continuous

Sedative, Hypnotic Abuse

Cannabis dependence, in remission

Tobacco dependence

History of Major Depressive Disorder, Recurrent

History of Generalized Anxiety Disorder

In the three days between her discharge from Eagleville and her assessment at Caron, her GAF score had dropped from 65 to 50. Her medical treatment plan stated the following:

Preliminary Treatment Plan

Problem #1: Dependence

Objective Findings: The patient's history endorses opiate dependence along with sedative, hypnotic abuse. There was a history of tolerance, withdrawal, substances taken in larger amounts over a longer period of time, loss of control, persistent desire to cut down, increased time spent using substance, loss of occupation, social and recreational activities secondary to use. Motivation to change seems mostly internal.

Goal: Long-term sobriety.

Plan: *Patient will be immersed in 12-Step relapse extended care programmatics* [emphasis mine].

Giana also had a psychological evaluation by a PhD psychologist who would continue to have some limited interaction with Giana during her stay. Listed under "Negative Factors That

May Affect Treatment" in the psychological assessment is the following sentence: "*Giana is a relapse patient and may not have fully grasped the 12-Step concepts including Step-One* [emphasis mine]." This statement suggests that rather than relapse being symptomatic of patients with OUD, Giana's relapses were due to her failure to understand and embrace the 12 Steps, particularly the notion of powerlessness in Step One.

By this point, Giana had been treated at Keystone, Valley Forge, Rehab After Work, Malvern, and Eagleville, yet the implication is that *she* had failed at getting well, rather than the iterative treatment being a failure.

The plan includes more detailed steps, phrased as agreements by Giana. So for example, under the "Problem 1.1: Patient's ability to make good decisions is impaired by lack of insight into the consequences of their choices, poor impulse control, or all-or-nothing thinking," some of the activities are:

- I will list 15 consequences of my disease and share on time in group
- I will complete a daily 10th step inventory sheet and turn it in to my counselor on a daily basis
- I will discuss how the concept of powerlessness relates to my use of drugs and alcohol
- I will discuss my definition of unmanageability and how it applies to me
- I will utilize local support through twelve step fellowships
- I will explain why I need a sponsor and how I will go about getting a sponsor

The 12-Step orientation of the program is very clear here, where all points except the first are explicitly linked to the 12 Steps. Regarding the first point, that Giana will make a list of the negative consequences, she had been given this exact assignment previously at Eagleville, and that list is among the papers she left behind from there. The problem with this assignment, wherever it is given, is that one of the characteristics of SUD is that people continue to use *despite negative consequences*. Yes, this is "powerlessness." However, listing and reciting negative consequences while in an enforced state of sobriety is unlikely to have much effect in overcoming powerlessness or, more importantly, the cravings, brain impairment, and underlying mental illness related to her relapses.

The following is one of three recommendations for Giana's treatment by this psychologist: "Giana does not have a spiritual foundation, and it will be important for her to learn to develop a connection with a Higher Power while she is here in treatment. Follow up with a spiritual counselor is highly recommended." Here is the suggestion that perhaps treatment has not been successful because Giana's spirituality is insufficient. The struggle to connect with a Higher Power occupied Giana during her entire four-month stay at Caron.

In my immediate family, there are people who identify as Catholic, mostly lapsed; Protestant, mostly lapsed; and Jewish, lapsed or nonreligious but observant. In Lou's family, everyone was Catholic, now mostly lapsed. Since early adulthood, Lou has been an outspoken atheist and highly critical of the Church, observing the Catholic rituals only when unavoidable, as in the last rites for his parents. I was never as confident or outspoken but did not see the relevance of organized religion in my life. I learned from my grandmother the possibility of being ethical without being religious. Giana received a liberal religious education by attending a Quaker school, where she studied ethics, took classes about all the major religions and a class about Quakerism, attended Quaker meeting weekly, and performed various types of service in the Quaker tradition. As a high school student, she used her swimming skills to provide support for severely disabled children in an adapted swimming pool. Of all our kids, she was the most outspoken atheist but also, by virtue of her interests, the one who understood, observed, and appreciated religious iconography in art and literature and most clearly understood the tangled knots of history and religion. But she had no religious faith.

In light of Giana's difficulties with the Higher Power, Lou and I have discussed whether we should have ignored our own beliefs and inclinations and raised the kids in church, leaving it to them to decide what they wanted to believe. Of course, we'll never know, but as with so many things, I'll always wonder. Giana was very comfortable with externally imposed structure. It made her feel secure and calmed her anxiety. She might have welcomed the timeless rituals of the Church, found the predictability soothing, even if she doubted deeply and rejected a number of the doctrines that are flashpoints in contemporary society. And then again she might have decided that she did not want to continue to be connected to the Church at all.

The Higher Power is a major obstacle about AA/NA for many patients. Step 2 states the need to "believe that a Power greater than ourselves could restore us to sanity." God is mentioned in five of the 12 steps, although in some AA/NA literature you will see God referred to as G-d, an attempt to communicate that the Higher Power doesn't have to be a traditional God. In recent years, as society has become increasingly more secular, the Higher Power (or HP, as it is often referred to in rehab) is sometimes reduced to anything the patient can believe is transcendent. In the end, many people, including Giana, find this to be disingenuous given the very Christian tilt of most AA/NA meetings, the use of the capitalized Him, and the message, repeated in various ways, that outside intervention from a force more powerful that oneself is needed for recovery.

Listed on the Media Center of the Caron website are descriptions of sessions from a workshop/lecture series called Spiritual Fridays, organized at the Caron Renaissance facility by the spiritual director, Reverend Laurie Durgan. Each Friday the group explores the relationship of spirituality to recovery, including "spiritual principles associated with each of the 12 steps." The accounts of these sessions are a testament to Caron's continuing endorsement of AA, especially the HP, as the core of its treatment approach.

Introducing the April 17, 2017, meeting, Rev. Durgan writes: "We walk into our first AA meeting with everything we need to stay sober—we just don't know it until we find each other and a Power greater than ourselves."

This is the endorsement of a startling concept: that the fellowship of AA meetings and a Higher Power are all that is needed for recovery. They are "everything"—evidently "we" don't need therapy, medication, or the many other treatments and interventions listed on the Caron website! A more ringing—and ironic—endorsement of AA principles would be hard to find.

At most of the rehabs, group sessions started with a reading from *Just for Today*, a book of daily meditations published in 1983 by Narcotics Anonymous World Services and widely available through Amazon and various booksellers. Here is an excerpt from one of the readings that Rev. Durgan references. "Ongoing recovery is dependent on our relationship with a loving G-d who cares for us and will do for us what we find impossible to do for ourselves. . . ." *Just for Today* (NA daily reader, April 30).

. . . *Do for us what we find impossible to do for ourselves.* Giana's atheism led to far-fetched attempts at various rehabs for her to find and accept her HP or risk being unable to recover. Sometimes her HP was her dogs, those dead and alive. At Caron, Giana's search to find her Higher Power resulted in an extensive effort to build animal totems. The spiritual counselor made this note during the third week of her stay at Caron: "Offered patient medicine cards, Earth-based meditation cards to use as a daily Step 11 process . . . Patient will journal which cards she received and look back at the entry at the end of the day to see if there was correlation with the message on the card." The following week the counselor wrote, "We discussed how she might look at each animal and see if she can apply one step of the 12-step program to each animal . . . Gave patient another book of totems to help her continue building her personal totem."

When Giana described this to me, I felt as if she was being treated with something akin to astrology. But she complied.

I have a notebook that Giana kept of this process. It was among the items she packed up and gave to me before she left Caron for The Rose House. In her dear neat printing, she made detailed notes, pages long, about each animal according to the card and then a list of the steps and how various animals had characteristics aligned with them.

Giana spent significant time trying to find something that would transcend self, which I think she interpreted as something larger than herself that would give purpose to her life and motivation for recovery. She and I discussed the concept of service to others, the way Martin Luther King spoke of it, as one such thing. However, according to the NA daily reading, the G-d of AA is a powerful supernatural being who can intervene to "do for us what we find impossible to do for ourselves." The Higher Power Giana was trying to build through animal totems or her love for her dogs clearly did not have the ability to do this, and Giana's treatment team remained frustrated by her failure. On November 25, less than three weeks before her discharge, her spiritual counselor made this note: "Patient still struggling with not having a conscious contact with her Higher Power."

In that notebook I found the following comments by you:

> *God: all knowing, all powerful forgiving, loving,*
> *tolerant, light w/in us (Quaker) works thru people . . .*
> *Not sure I believe any of the above.*
> *Ideas:*
> *Nature*
> *Animals, animal spirits— Maggie and Abby*
> *The universe*
> *The ocean (water)*

Later in the notebook you say: "I don't believe God created earth and humans. I don't believe God watches over you and takes care of you and that everything happens for a reason and God only gives you as much as you can handle . . . I am willing to believe or trying to believe in a power greater than myself. I didn't make the universe, I can't control nature. I believe those things and animals are a greater power than me. But I'm still having a hard time connecting to that."

You and Dad and I talked a lot about the Higher Power. The difficulty, I think, was the idea of surrendering to something that, while you couldn't control it, you didn't believe had any particular interest in you. You believed that the flow of nature, while outside of your control, is indifferent to you and can indeed be destructive, not necessarily caring or loving. Therefore, how can surrendering to it—indifferent and sometimes destructive—be positive? And how can you pray to it, trust in it, and depend on it, as comments in your notebook by your spiritual counselor advise you to do?

"Over the River and through the Wood"—a poem I used to read to my children as we prepared for Thanksgiving. Well, this was not quite that, but it reminded me of the poem. I couldn't give anyone route numbers or street names, but once off the turnpike, you turn at the auction mart, always closed on Sunday, then shoot out a rolling exurb road where there is a trusting stand at which you can buy firewood by putting money in a can and taking the wood you want. Then a right at the pizza store and a left at the house with the hex sign on it. Soon Caron's white fences come into view.

While Giana was at Caron, Lou and I drove to see her every Sunday, usually together. I looked forward to those drives, and those Sundays were precious to both of us. Giana's illness had brought us closer, but we had been on warm terms for a long time. Grandchildren have a way of doing that. We spent the drive, usually an hour or so, chatting about those grandchildren, our children, our other family members, and our many mutual interests—books, movies, travel, politics, and tennis.

Most Sundays with Giana we went out to lunch, roamed around Barnes and Noble and bought books, and often went to a movie. Sometimes we took Giana to pick up toiletries or clothes. We both wanted to grill her about everything that she was doing at Caron, mostly to reassure ourselves that she was getting better, but we tried to limit treatment talk. Mostly we just wanted to enjoy our daughter. It was a relief and joy to be with her and not to wonder if she was high or planning to get high. While some days she was in a brighter mood than others, her depression was still apparent. But every Sunday she looked better, the dark smudges under her eyes lighter and her skin clearer.

Toward the end of September, Lou and I attended the Caron Family Education Program (FEP), a four-day event. This time we drove up separately, as I was staying a day longer; he had to return to work and miss the final day. Lou had booked us (separate) rooms at a nearby bed and breakfast, so close to

Caron we could have walked had we wanted to. The FEP was something we had been informed about at the time of Giana's admission. This type of program is common at high-end residential rehabs. According to Fletcher: "Residential rehabs commonly offer 'psychoeducational' family weeks wherein relatives attend lectures and have peer-group discussions to learn about the disease of addiction, the twelve steps, and Al-Anon support groups for family members of people with addictions" (137).

The four-day Caron program followed this model. From the Caron website:

Our Adult Family Education Program enables family members to learn about addiction, including how addiction progresses and the ways relationships are affected.

The topics to be covered in the Adult Family Education Program include:

- Addiction as a progressive disease
- The impact of addiction
- Enabling behaviors vs. healthy boundaries
- Introduction to recovery and 12-Step programming
- Relapse behaviors
- Effective communication
- Recovery action plans
- Enabling addiction vs. supporting recovery
- Relapse as a part of the disease process
- Detaching with love
- Establishing and maintaining boundaries
- Communication styles
- The role of each individual in achieving wellness (August 2017)

The four days began on Saturday morning with introductions and an overview of the program. There were about twenty people present, mostly parents but some spouses, seated in a large circle. Our loved ones had a wide range of substance use, from alcohol to cocaine to methamphetamine to benzodiazepines to opioids to combinations. The facilitator was a "lead therapist," a master's-level professional. We went around the room and explained what we would like to get out of the program. The woman sitting next to me started crying when it was her turn to speak. I put my hand on her shoulder to comfort her, and the facilitator politely told me not to do this. I must have given her an inquiring look, for she explained that it was important to let the woman "sit with her feelings." This has to do with allowing oneself—and evidently others—to feel uncomfortable feelings in therapy. But this is not what I thought this session was about—this was not a group therapy session, was it? I was both offended and confused. I could not then and do not now understand what is wrong with one bereft parent comforting another; in some topsy-turvy pop psychology universe, compassion is somehow interpreted as inappropriate.

Actually, I believe the facilitators did view this as "group therapy" even though it was billed as "family education." I think this response occurred because the facilitator and other staff encountered over the four days seemed to think that all the family members there were in fact unwell and needed to "do their own work" in their own 12-Step "recovery process" in a group such as AA or NA. These are 12-Step support groups for family members of alcoholics and those with dependency or addiction to various drugs. From the therapist's notes: ". . . in the AM, discussion was on the Twelve Steps, what integration of these principles into one's daily life means, detaching with love and boundaries." There was an assumption that we were all trying to control our loved ones and that we needed to learn to set boundaries because we were enabling their addictions. We needed to detach. This was preparation for the focus throughout the program on setting boundaries and dealing with codependency.

Codependency is a word you hear a lot in recovery programs. Related ideas have been bounced around since the sixties and seventies, but its popularity harkens back to a best-selling self-help book titled *Codependent No More*, published in 1986. In a general sense, it usually means that one person depends too much on another and fails to be independent enough, and the person being depended upon gets inappropriate satisfaction from the dependency of the other. Thus, both people are unwell. The idea in recovery programs is that the person with substance use disorder relies upon a family member who enables the addiction in various ways and keeps the addicted person from getting well. One of the exercises in the FEP on that first day was this: ". . . each family member shared their family of origin history with their peers in order to find the 'emotional hook', which allows them to give into the patients when they are in their active addiction and further enable the disease." I have no recollection of what we said, but I assume it had something to do with Giana's history of various illnesses.

There is no listing in the DSM V for "codependency." It is not recognized as a form of mental illness like a mood disorder or a substance use disorder or anorexia. It's basically just a popular idea that the 12-Step recovery community seized upon and twisted to fit its idea of SUD and how it should be treated, which includes the idea that addiction is a "family disease" and the people who are not actually using have to be in their own program to recover from codependency and enabling. Much of the AA-based rhetoric about boundaries and codependence, which made me uneasy then, seems absolutely wrongheaded to me now. I think about the medical problem that was developing at this time with my mother, an illness that required continual care and support of all kinds, an illness that required shared decision making, and I wonder what the difference is. Giana needed continual care, help with decision making, transport to treatments and financial help with them, and love—which is just what my mother needed. Is this difference of viewpoint because the 12-Step–based recovery system doesn't really view SUD as a chronic, relapsing illness like other medical conditions, such as lupus, or mental health diseases, such as bipolar disorder, and thus doesn't believe it should be treated in the same way?

The second day of FEP began with a chapel service. It wasn't mandatory, but since Giana was going as part of her diligent effort to connect to her Higher Power, we went also. Caron has a large chapel with comfortable seating, which I suppose is also used for other types of assemblies. The service was a mix of Christian practice, music, 12-Step references, and testimonials to Caron and to recovery. I think there was guitar playing. Patients were not permitted to sit with family members, so we sat a couple rows behind Giana. She seemed very comfortable with her fellow patients, smiling at friends and turning occasionally to smile at us.

The rest of the day was spent with family members and patients in lectures and small group discussions about boundaries and codependency. A Caron alumnus and his wife, who, according to the notes, was "recovering in Al-anon," spoke to the group. The small group discussions were interesting, mostly because I got to meet the friends Giana had talked about. It was a good day because we got to spend it with Giana. In the notes, the therapist summed it up this way: "It also seemed that family members were beginning to gain some insight into their codependency and the reality that each have [*sic*] their own work to do." I find that this observation differs from my recollection. I remember one father who stated very calmly that he was at FEP to support his wife and daughter, that he had already accepted that his daughter might eventually die from her substance use, and that he simply wanted to spend as much time with her as he possibly could. I do not think this father felt he needed direction in how to address his codependency. Lou and I had tried out various support groups, including AA, and found them unhelpful. In the several 12-Step groups we attended, the emphasis on a traditional Christian God was ubiquitous and not in line with our thinking or beliefs. We were already seeing a therapist, both together and separately, with the goal of providing the best support we could for Giana and keeping our anxieties and sorrow from overwhelming us and our other children. We had intentionally picked a therapist whose background included clinical work in a residential rehab; we did not think of this as "our own work to do" in the way the lead therapist implied, nor did we see the need or relevance of adopting the 12 Steps as our touchstone. There were a number of like-minded family members.

In a small group the next morning, Giana presented an "addiction timeline," which illustrated the extent of her use from high school to the present. While Lou and I were surprised by the frequency of high school and college drinking and the use of benzodiazepines in the preceding five years, in general we were familiar with what we heard. The benefit of the exercise, if there was one, would have been that Giana had been dishonest in large and small ways as her addiction became more severe, and this demonstration of honesty with us was meant to lay new ground for our relationship. The thing is that in the past, whenever she had decided to seek help, she talked with me very openly. It was only when she was in active addiction and resisting treatment that she lied. So for her to present this timeline to us after having been sober for ten weeks or more didn't seem like much of a departure from previous patterns.

That afternoon Lou left, and Giana had a pass to spend time with me. She came back to the bed and breakfast, and we sat in my very pleasant room and talked for a while, mostly about her recent breakup with M. She had been ambivalent about the relationship off and on for a while, but she had also pushed so many people out of her life that her connection to him was almost the only one she had left, apart from family. In general our family was negative about the relationship, although I was sympathetic at times because Giana was so lonely and so sad. M quickly became an issue at Caron, where staff and peers saw the relationship as unhealthy and a barrier to Giana's recovery.

With prodding, Giana had ended the relationship over the phone about two weeks before the Family Education Program, with support in the room from her addiction counselor and several of her friends. At the time of our conversation, she felt that she had made the right decision but was intermittently sad and guilty about it. M would be an ongoing theme during Giana's stay at Caron, exacerbated by Giana's disclosures that she answered an email from him and then wrote him a letter that she shredded instead of mailing. These actions were termed "relapse behavior." I agreed that ending the relationship was necessary. However, when I read the notes and see how much it was discussed in various sessions, and even in case consults, I am puzzled. Giana was disclosing to everyone how anxious and depressed she felt. On her daily Tenth-Step worksheets, in answer to the question about what "negative thoughts" she had that day, there is almost always an answer such as the one of October 21 that reads "anxiety, depression, sadness, remorse" or the one from November 11 that reads "anxiety, sadness, grief" or from November 18, less than a month before her discharge: "worried about future, anxiety." As I read these, alarm bells ring. Clearly her depression and anxiety were not lessening, and while breaking up with M may have been necessary for her future recovery, in that moment it was exacerbating her feelings of sadness. Yet in the notes, no one comes forth and hollers, "This woman is not improving! Her mental health is a huge relapse risk! What should we do?" The drumbeat of groups and more groups went on as usual.

This issue of groups versus individual therapy or counseling comes up frequently in writing about rehab. Obviously groups are more cost effective. But are they therapeutically effective? Fletcher says, "I also wondered whether there's scientific evidence that group treatment is an effective way to help people with substance use disorder. Like so many things in this field, despite widespread use, group therapy for addiction has not been well researched and we know little about its effectiveness" (214). Certainly groups are better for some people than others, and certainly they cannot be expected to adequately address co-occuring disorders such as major depression. Well-known addiction experts such as A. Thomas McLellan, PhD, and Dr. Mark Willenbring have repeatedly advocated for more individual work in treatment.

After a while, Giana and I left the bed and breakfast and went for a long walk. That day she was talkative and accessible. The blank wall that she sometimes presented was not there as we walked through an area of small farms and clusters of homes, cattle grazing here and there, and a slow-moving stream beside the windy road. There were no sidewalks, but there was also very little traffic. We caught up about the doings of various cousins and talked for a bit about the FEP. This was Giana's fifth residential stay, on top of several stints in PHP and IOP. We'd been over most of the FEP content many times. We spent the rest of the walk talking about a sculptor. I laughed when she asked me if I knew David Smith's work. Uh, yeah . . . do you remember the National Gallery? You went there with me!

Throughout FEP there was a lot of talk about relapse behavior, relapse risks, and the relapse process. This included the need to determine high-risk situations and triggers and the development of relapse prevention plans: when triggered, call a friend, call your sponsor, take a walk, take a bath, and so forth. Giana had relapsed after Keystone, after Valley Forge, after Malvern. She was being given the same tools. Why would one expect a different outcome?

At no time during the FEP was there any information or discussion about medication.

~

Caron seems to have had an uncomfortable relationship with harm reduction and medication-assisted treatment for some time.

In 2007 Doug Tieman, Caron's CEO, wrote an article entitled "In Support of Abstinence" in the journal *Behavioral Healthcare Executive*. Here Mr. Tieman states that while there is a role for harm reduction strategies, ultimately abstinence is the only way to have a better life. When Giana was in treatment at Caron, addiction medication was not a standard part of their treatment and was not promoted on the website or to the patient and family members alongside 12-Step principles, addiction counseling, cognitive behavioral therapy, and other interventions. I would argue that if medication-assisted treatment rather than abstinence had been a mainstay of Caron's program (or at other facilities before she ever got to Caron), she now might have a life that she could work on making better.

On September 26, 2016, Caron published a statement on its website by Joseph Garbely, a psychiatrist and Caron Pennsylvania's medical director, acknowledging the opioid epidemic as a crisis and endorsing the use of Vivitrol, which had been approved by the FDA in 2010. The statement stresses that "medication alone is not a panacea" and goes on to emphasize the importance of other treatment practices, including the 12 Steps. Vivitrol is the injectable, extended-release form of naltrexone and was no doubt preferred by Caron because it is an opioid anti-agonist, not a partial agonist like methadone and buprenorphine. You cannot manipulate naltrexone to get high.

Those who believe that abstinence without medication is ideal often see medication as substituting one drug for another. This is an anachronistic approach to treatment that simply runs counter to current evidence that medication-assisted treatment produces the best results. NIDA, in a 2016 brief titled "Effective Treatments for Opioid Addiction," addresses this bias. It says: "Methadone and buprenorphine do not substitute one addiction for another. When someone is treated for an opioid addiction, the dosage of medication used does not get them high—it helps reduce opioid cravings and withdrawal. These medications restore balance to the brain circuits affected by addiction, allowing the patient's brain to heal while working toward recovery."

On July 20, 2017, Caron posted a revised policy statement on MAT. The new policy included the use of buprenorphine maintenance as a choice if Caron's primary choice, Vivitrol, was not advised for a particular patient, although apparently the patient would need to have it prescribed by a doctor outside of Caron. The statement includes the same warning about medication not being a "panacea." At this point, one had to search to find this statement about MAT on Caron's website. It was buried in a section called "Treatment Philosophy," under a subsection called "We Treat the Mind, the Body, and the Spirit." Under the "Body" section, "medication, if necessary" was part of a list of methods that also include exercise and fitness, as well as nutrition.

On March 9, 2018, Caron again revised its policy. Due to "the prescription opioid and heroin epidemic we are currently facing as a society," Caron now endorses the use of all three of the medications, although apparently does not provide methadone at their facilities. That "medication alone is not a panacea" is still prominent in the statement. The statement stresses that other approaches, such as CBT and dialectical behavioral therapy (DBT), must be employed to address co-occurring disorders that are so common to those with opioid addiction. One hopes that they are employed with greater fidelity and more systematically than they were when Giana was at Caron. Of course there is still acknowledgment of 12-Step integration.

But now MAT is included prominently in the listing of interventions, a step forward.

I assume that the welcome evolution of Caron's position on MAT has something to do with recent research, and may also be related to patient input and requests. It may also have something to do with a shifting public and private insurance landscape, where there is a slow move toward only funding treatment that includes MAT because the evidence of its efficacy is so convincing. It's tragic that Caron, with its significant regional footprint and national reputation, did not take the lead in endorsing and promoting MAT. All three medications were FDA approved years before Giana got to Caron, and at that time there was positive evidence from rigorous research. If MAT had been an integral part of the Caron treatment protocol when Giana was there, she would have had a greater chance at remission.

Apparently Caron patients used naltrexone during the time Giana was at Caron. When Giana checked in, she was placed in a unit called "Women's Extended Care," which served adult women, generally for a three-month period. Among the many papers that Giana left behind from Caron is a thick binder called "Adult Handbook," which appears to be some sort of combination of manual and workbook. It has many places for the patient to make notes: pages to make notes from educational lectures, pages to make notes about "step work," grids to comment on the effectiveness of alternative treatments such as yoga, whirlpool, and meditation. For reasons that are unclear, Giana did not make notes anywhere in this book; however, there are some similar exercises on individual worksheets elsewhere in her papers.

There are several references to medication in the Adult Handbook. In the section entitled "Medications Used in Substance Withdrawal," there is an explanation about medications used in detoxification. The section ends with this: "Buprenorphine is used in many treatment programs as a long-term drug to avoid relapsing onto narcotics. Caron uses this medication short-term only and advises you to use 12-Step support, Naltrexone, and strong personal relapse prevention as a method to handle cravings" (79). Stuck into a sleeve on the inside front cover of the handbook, I found a pharmaceutical company handout about Vivitrol.

The progress notes from Caron show that the day after her arrival she was seen and examined by a doctor. An LPN also made the following note:

The patient stated that they reviewed the Vivitrol information that is in the admission binder and the patient is interested/not interested at this time. An appointment will be scheduled with MD/NP to discuss it further. (August 15, 2013)

Neither "interested" nor "not interested" is circled or marked, so Giana's wishes on this are impossible to know.

I don't know what kind of discussion Giana may have had with this LPN about Vivitrol. She certainly never mentioned it to her father or me, and it is not noted anywhere in her initial treatment plan. For a person who had already had several documented relapses, I have to wonder why Vivitrol was not a standard part of her treatment toolkit, begun as soon as she entered so she would be used to the monthly protocol when she left as prevention against future relapse. I think about one of the patients in Giana's group who relapsed on a weekend home pass to see her young daughter; the use of Vivitrol would have prevented that. I think back to the easy availability of heroin at Malvern—what if all fully detoxed patients had been given a shot of Vivitrol there? Would Giana have accepted heroin when it was offered to her there if she knew that she would feel no effect from it? One can't know, but instead of offering the protective buffer of Vivitrol, Malvern failed to prevent heroin from being smuggled in and then kicked her out for using it.

This reference to Vivitrol is the last one in the Caron notes regarding medication for addiction until October 22, when Giana refused naltrexone when it was offered to her with her daily meds, stating that she was not aware that she was starting the medication. Later that day Giana had a session with her addiction counselor, who wrote this note: "I asked Giana about her refusal of naltrexone this morning, and she stated that she did not speak with anyone from medical staff regarding this medication and was surprised when it was offered to her this morning. She stated her willingness to have a discussion with medical staff around the benefits of this medication, which will be relayed to medical staff."

Almost a month later, on November 19, there is a note by the LPN that Giana has been prescribed naltrexone and information about the drug has been reviewed with her. But in an amended treatment plan, dated November 20, it is stated: "Giana will follow up with medical staff around pharmacologic intervention and [*sic*] she approaches treatment completion. . . ."

Giana came to my mother's for two nights over Thanksgiving. A medical note dated November 27 lists the medications packed for her, and they did not include naltrexone. The medical records that show her daily medications never mention naltrexone after this prescription on November 19, nor is there an indication that she was offered it and refused.

In her medical discharge summary, the physician reports that Giana has no medical complaint but "she [Giana] does state that she continues to struggle with her depression but this seems to be getting a little bit better." She also says that Giana "was not interested in any type of anti-craving medication, as she did not feel that it would be helpful for her." Apparently naltrexone in pill or shot form was offered to Giana upon discharge. In light of Giana's relapse history and her persistent depression and anxiety, my conclusion here is that Giana was leaving the door open to use once she left Caron. Giana was well aware of naltrexone's ability to block heroin, having been prescribed it previously by her psychiatrist. It's quite perplexing that a treatment facility could not divine such an obvious motive. Vivitrol should have been part of her treatment plan from her initial assessment, reinforced consistently throughout her stay at Caron, and then included as part of the protocol in My First Year, Caron's aftercare program.

Giana holding her infant nephew

Chapter Fourteen

During the time between my mother's delayed "annual" visit and her diagnosis, a period of about eight weeks during which Giana was at Caron, my mother's life was quite the same as it had been. No longer driving, she often went out on errands or to lunch with one or another of her younger friends. We kids saw her frequently, but not daily, and checked in by phone. She continued to do what she liked, which included watching tennis on TV. One night during the US Open, we all repeatedly tried to reach her, but she wasn't answering her phone. Finally at eleven thirty my sister jumped in her car, drove the thirty minutes to my mother's apartment, and burst in the door. My mother was sitting calmly on the sofa, watching Nadal, her favorite. "Oh," she said, "I guess I left the phone somewhere." We were always more worried about her than she was about herself.

In late August my mother's doctor received the results of her blood panel. Apparently he misread the tests and suggested that she see a cardiologist. In fact she had already been seeing one, my late stepfather's doctor. Up to that point, my mother had no major heart problems and was medicated only for high blood pressure. She used to go with my stepfather to see this doctor; he was quite a character, and they always came home with funny stories. I went with her to the appointment. The doctor came flying into the room, hands waving the blood test results. "There's nothing wrong with your heart," he cried. "You have no blood!"

I had no idea what he meant, but he arranged for us to see a hematologist the next day. From that point on, my brother the doctor took over interacting with the doctors. Several weeks of testing later, my mother had a diagnosis of myelodysplastic syndrome, a disease sometimes called "preleukemia," which is characterized by a lack of mature red blood cells. After deciding against a clinical trial she was offered, outpatient treatment was scheduled to begin closer to home. The treatment plan consisted of blood transfusions to keep her blood count up, and subcutaneous injections of mild chemotherapy drugs. We were to be careful about germs, as she would be more susceptible to infections. I remember discussing with my siblings what that meant. Clean more? Wipe down everything every day with disinfectant? Limit visitors? No way! She wanted to see people! Don't let her go anywhere? I was so opposed to that. She was still alive—let her live. She could go to the movies and wear a protective mask. People in Japan do it every day on the subway!

I never asked for a prognosis; perhaps my brother knew, but he never said. In retrospect, until two weeks before she died, I never thought my mother's death was imminent. I took no steps to talk to her further about a funeral—we had agreed long ago that she would be cremated—or to begin going through her amazing horde of family memorabilia, china, silver, Christmas decorations, and jewelry. Was this out of fear? I don't think so. This is the person I used to be, the glass-half-full person, the person who always saw the silver lining, the person who thought that this illness was an impairment of my mother's quality of life but not a sign that she was dying any time soon. Hadn't her mother lived to 103?

My mother's first hospitalization occurred in early October and lasted for three weeks. She had reacted violently to the initial drug treatment and was much weakened. My brother T stopped in to check on her and found her almost unconscious. She had been sick all night, it appeared. She was in the ICU for a few days, followed by several weeks in a step-down unit. Even in the ICU, we were joking around with her; when she would awaken, we would ask her if she recognized everybody in the room. She usually did, but for some reason she kept forgetting one of my brothers. "Mom, he's the one who used to ride his bike on the roof!"

"Oh yes," she would say.

I went to the hospital every afternoon, able to make up work by staying later in the evenings, Giana safely tucked away at Caron. I was definitely taken aback by how weak my mother was. She had difficulty rising from a chair without help. She was taking a daily nap. However, they had a physical therapist coming to her room, and slowly she started to improve. She waved away the television most of the time and asked for newspapers and magazines. She wanted me to get a hairdresser in there. Displaying her amazing talent for connecting with people, she knew the life story of all the nurses and technicians, and I often found someone in there chatting with her.

Fortuitously, Louisa and her husband were scheduled to come to Philly during this period for a wedding. We scheduled a family reunion in my mother's hospital room: my kids, two spouses, and four grandsons. Lou went up and got Giana from Caron for the day, so he was there as well. The photographs I have reflect various people sitting next to my mother's hospital bed, grandsons piled on laps, and my mother looking surprisingly pretty for someone just out of ICU and wearing an oxygen feeder! Giana looks great in those pictures, smiling, happy, and warmly accessible. I remember being in the cafeteria and watching her banter back and forth with her siblings. It seemed so normal.

At some point, my brother the doctor and his wife showed up too. The hospital put up with us all day as we moved from the hospital room to a lounge area to the cafeteria and back. My oldest grandson brought my mother, a renowned cook and baker, a handmade card with a note that said, in red and green marker: "Grandmom, I hope you feel better because . . . I love pie! and I love you a lot! and You are my only great! and I love all the food you make! and You are forever young!" We taped this to the hospital window.

Louisa and her husband drove Giana back to Caron that evening and headed back to Colorado the next day; this trip was the last time Louisa saw her grandmother.

While Giana seemed well at the hospital reunion, my mother's illness was weighing on her. She asked anxiously about my mother whenever we communicated, and there are frequent references in the Caron notes to Giana's worry and sadness about my mother.

In mid-October, Giana's addiction counselor began talking to her about attending Caron's five-day Breakthrough program. On its website Caron describes Breakthrough as an intensive experiential program, based on attachment theory, using group techniques in a therapeutic community setting. It is not limited to Caron patients but serves the general public as well. It focuses on addressing low self-esteem, insecurity in relationships, and problems with emotional self-regulation, all of which were relevant to Giana. In the Adult Handbook, Breakthrough is written to be for "individuals who have ongoing problems with relationships and/or emotional conflicts that are interfering with their ability to lead fully healthy and productive lives."

Regarding Breakthrough's results, Caron's website at the time stated: "At the end of 5 days in an experiential group, clients have not only reached an awareness of their issues. They feel more confident; know who they are and they love themselves. They have begun to better manage their emotions, particularly fear and shame." On the website now are the results of a study done with Rutgers University showing positive results for most Breakthrough clients over a one year period.

In the treatment notes, there is no discussion of the reasons or expected outcomes leading up to the decision to offer this program to Giana, nor whether the techniques used were a good fit for her. However, the website at the time said: "The general goal for most clients is to improve quality of life by examining the 'how' of their struggles rather than the 'why' they struggle. When the past is relevant, Breakthrough professionals will dip into the past to shed light on current issues or to reduce shame." My assumption is that two primary factors led staff to recommend Breakthrough for Giana: her inability to completely let go of her relationship with M and her history of difficult and painful relationships, perhaps seen through the lens of the various problems resulting for her from Lou's and my chaotic relationship and eventual divorce.

What happened while Giana was there? Here's what the Breakthrough Workshop Summary for Giana said:

Giana attended:

- Lectures on attachment wounds and the resulting survival decisions which impact current behavior and struggles
- A guided imagery
- A silent family sculpture
- An exercise on managing painful feelings, followed by a letter sharing (parents) session
- A grief and loss exercise

Summary of Results: "Giana began to relate to how her tendency towards inwardness represented a retreat into herself based on early attempts to avoid frustration and emotional pain." She was able to "offer herself compassion and forgiveness." Giana also asked to work on letting go of her compulsive behaviors, and "with the same compassion and sorrow, severed ties with her internal world."

The continuing care plan that was recommended after Breakthrough included:

- Let go of "that which she has outgrown" and "develop compassion for herself and to practice forgiveness"
- "Recall feeling safe in her body; continue to enhance this safety by practicing restorative yoga"
- "Each day read the list of qualities that she discovered about her true essence; commit to the concept of inherit [*sic*] worth and value"
- Cultivate a relationship with herself
- Practice "you spot it, you got it." [This is a technique used in life coaching that suggests that when you see qualities in another that you dislike, they are probably qualities that you yourself have.]
- "Recall that attraction equals danger, and that her love template will need to be rewired to seek safety as opposed to danger/chaos"

I spoke with Giana shortly after her Breakthrough experience, which concluded on November 1, and she was quite positive about it. She talked about how she had gotten in touch with her "inner child" and felt remorse at how she had disappointed the dreams and potential of that child. She did not speak to me about the exercises that explored her relationship with her father and me, if there were any, although she and I had spoken about these issues many, many times.

Unfortunately, after an initial boost to her mood, she experienced a slide into deeper depression. There is caution in the discharge instructions from Breakthrough about feeling tender and vulnerable in the weeks following Breakthrough, and a recommendation for "outpatient therapy," which must have been a generic prescription, since, of course, they knew she was a residential patient. However, the treatment notes do not reflect any changes in Giana's schedule to provide for individual sessions to process her experience. Her next appointment with the psychologist took place a full two weeks after her discharge from Breakthrough. Even though there was evidence of worsening depression, it doesn't appear that an alarm bell was sounded.

A few days after Breakthrough's conclusion, on November 4, her addiction counselor made the following note about her participation in group: "She was able to share some confusion around her feelings upon completion of the Breakthrough program."

On November 7, Giana saw the psychiatrist. He notes, "Giana's mood was described as sad and anxious today." However, he states that she feels a benefit from Breakthrough. He increased the dosage of Abilify.

On November 8, Giana had an individual session with her addiction counselor, who wrote: "We spoke about her experience in Breakthrough last week and some of the struggles she is having. Giana spoke about feeling apathetic toward treatment and expressed 'boredom and depression' as her main feelings this week. She spoke about 'not caring' what other people have to say and her projections about the future. She expressed hopelessness and a desire to be relieved of her current state." The response to this is the following: "Giana will continue to participate in Women's Extended Care scheduled programming. She will complete treatment assignments and will present these interventions in group or individual sessions." Apparently her addiction counselor didn't feel the need to consult with her supervisor, the psychologist, or the psychiatrist about Giana's state of mind.

On November 14, Giana saw the psychologist. It appears to be a routine check-in following their last individual session on October 9. The note says: "Giana describes feeling apathetic and anhedonic. We talked about where this is coming from currently." There is no mention of Breakthrough or her experience there, so there is no way to know if it was discussed. She concludes: "Giana continues to struggle with depressed mood and symptoms of depression." The psychologist's plan is to "monitor via team in in [*sic*] mileu [*sic*]."

Looking back at Giana's initial assessments, there appears to be no concrete plan to treat her disorders of anxiety and depression. In her initial assessment, the psychologist recommended that a psychiatrist evaluate Giana's current medication and stated that she may "benefit from periodic follow-up with the unit psychologist to *monitor* [emphasis mine] her depression and anxiety. . . ."

Earlier in her assessment, this psychologist noted that "it does not appear that her co-occurring disorders had been adequately addressed in prior treatments." With this I wholeheartedly agree. What I cannot understand, then, is why she recommends "periodic follow-up" to "monitor" Giana's depression and anxiety rather than a treatment plan for her depression and anxiety. After all, Caron's website stated: "Drug and alcohol problems are rarely isolated. They go hand-in-hand with co-occurring disorders, like depression, anxiety, trauma-related disorders, and eating disorders, to name just a few. At Caron, we address these issues together with substance abuse, because treatment of co-occurring disorders is vital to patients' success in treatment and long-term sobriety" (March 2017).

The initial treatment plan does not address any specific treatment for Giana's depression and anxiety, her co-occurring disorders. It does recommend participation in four "specialty" groups: Seeking Safety, Family of Origin, Body Image, and Opiate Group. Other groups were added during her stay. Among her papers from Caron, I did find a seventeen-page handout on depression, copied from the National Institute of Mental Health. Perhaps somebody felt that reading about it might help?

The psychologist began "monitoring" Giana's depression and anxiety when, fourteen days after Giana's admission, on August 28, the psychologist saw her in an individual session. This professional never indicated the time or duration of sessions, so it is impossible to know how long they spoke. Giana described herself as more depressed than upon admission, and the psychologist agreed, writing, "Giana's mood is depressed and affect is flat." She notes that Giana is withdrawn "and is not active in groups." Thus, she recommends that Giana should participate in an additional group, the AID (Addiction Interaction Disorder) specialty group, "given her history of ED [eating disorders] and dysfunctional relationships." The psychologist refers her to the psychiatrist.

Giana saw the psychiatrist for the first time on August 30 in a session that also served as an initial assessment. He added Abilify to her set of medications, to boost the performance of Cymbalta.

Giana's interaction with the psychologist and psychiatrist followed this routine throughout her stay at Caron, seeing the psychologist individually a total of four times in the four months she was there, in addition to her initial assessment. Generally these sessions followed a pattern where Giana states how she is feeling and the psychologist comments in the notes. The only topic ever discussed in a substantive, recurring fashion was Giana's ongoing attachment to her boyfriend, M. Giana saw the psychiatrist more frequently, generally every one to three weeks, for what amounted to a medication check. Over time he increased the Abilify to 10 mg and eventually discontinued it when Giana began to refuse it, saying that it made her anxious. There is also no indication of the duration of these sessions.

Meanwhile the psychologist included Giana in a few groups

of dialectical behavioral therapy, a type of cognitive behavioral therapy originally designed for people with borderline personality disorder and suicidal tendencies, but adopted in a casual way in many rehab facilities. This group met five or six times during Giana's stay; sometimes groups were not specifically identified in the notes, and it's difficult to tell what they were. In addition, the psychologist conducted mindfulness meditation with Giana's primary counseling group on an almost weekly basis. And even though Giana was already in a Body Image group, the psychologist included Giana in a new group she started for people with current and past eating disorders.

On our weekend visits, Giana described some of the groups and what they were for, but even she seemed overwhelmed by them and sometimes unable to articulate just what the purpose of a certain group was compared to another. Often she had to leave one group before it was over to go to another group. She expressed that it was exhausting and that she didn't feel that she was making much progress. She was depressed, and she still had strong cravings. When someone in her unit relapsed on a weekend home visit, Giana told us that although she was sorry to say it, the reaction she had was jealousy. At about two and a half months, I asked Giana's addiction counselor when they were going to start addressing some of the things from Giana's past in therapy. "We're getting there" was the response. But in fact they never got there.

The point is that Giana received no systematic, regularly planned, individualized therapy for her co-occurring mental health disorders while she was at Caron. Neither the individual nor group sessions with her addiction counselor, who held a BA, were therapy—they were addiction counseling. This person was not a therapist. In Pennsylvania regulatory language, therapists are as follows: a licensed professional counselor (LPC), which requires a master's degree, an exam, and supervised work experience; or a licensed marriage and family therapist (LMFT), which requires at least a master's degree and supervised work experience; or a licensed psychologist, which requires a doctorate and supervised work experience.

For Giana there were mental health problems that were either ignored or mismanaged throughout her treatment in every facility, including Caron. These problems were her "co-occurring" disorders (previously referred to as dual diagnoses), namely major depressive disorder and generalized anxiety disorder. Most clinicians added her serious eating disorder history. People with mental health disorders are more likely than people without these to experience substance use disorder. While it is true that people struggling with SUD often experience depression and anxiety, Giana's mental health problems had been diagnosed years before and were not symptoms of her drug use but contributors to it. Nevertheless, her depression and anxiety were largely ignored in her many rehab stays. Unfortunately this is typical and well-documented. The CASA report states:

"In standard medical practice, it is recommended that health professionals assess the presence of co-occurring conditions in order to develop an effective treatment plan and tailor treatment accordingly. Although such assessments are critical in addiction treatment given the very high rate of co-occurring conditions in people with addiction, treatment programs frequently do not address co-occurring health conditions or do so in a suboptimal way. Implementing a one-size-fits-all approach to treatment based solely on a clinical diagnosis without consideration of co-occurring health conditions often amounts to a waste of time and resources." (209)

Given the treatment plan, it seems that some of the specialty groups were thought to take the place of therapy. Giana should have been receiving one-on-one therapy at least twice if not three times a week for her entire stay. Over four months that would have been somewhere between thirty-two and forty-eight sessions. Instead, she had four sessions. Rather than resources invested in highly credentialed and experienced staff, lesser qualified staff ran groups for eight to twelve people instead.

One of these was called "Seeking Safety." According to a handout among Giana's papers, Seeking Safety is a treatment for trauma/PTSD and "substance abuse" consisting of twenty-five "psychotherapy" topics. It was first published in 2002 and can be purchased as a manual from a variety of places, including Amazon and Barnes and Noble. The following is a description from the website Treatment Innovations, connected to Seeking Safety:

"Seeking Safety is an evidence-based, present focused counseling model to help people attain safety from trauma and/or substance abuse. It can be conducted in group (any size) and/or individual modality. It is an extremely safe model as it directly addresses both the trauma and the addiction, but without requiring clients to delve into the trauma narrative (the detailed account of disturbing trauma memories), thus making it relevant to a very broad range of clients and easy to implement. Any provider can conduct it even without training; however, there are also many options for training. It has also been delivered successfully by peers in addition to professionals of all kinds and in all settings. It can be conducted over any number of sessions available although the more the better when possible."

Thus, Seeking Safety appears to be an extremely flexible and inexpensive tool because it is easily purchased and photocopied (as Giana's handouts were); facilitators need no professional credentials whatsoever, even though they are delivering "psychotherapy topics"; it can be conducted in any size group; and the program or facilitator can pick and choose among the sessions and deliver them in no particular sequence. In other words, I could purchase it from Amazon and deliver it myself. Giana's Caron folder with "Seeking Safety" written in her hand across the front contains a number of photocopied handouts that indicate that they are from the 2002 manual. They are clearly copies of copies of copies, with the print faint and distorted in a way that indicates this. From a Caron-generated sheet in the folder, it is apparent that several of the twenty-five topics were bundled together for use in single sessions.

The handout in Giana's materials about Seeking Safety describes trauma as a "severe life event, such as physical or sexual abuse, a car accident, or a hurricane." Initially I wondered what event in Giana's life occasioned her participation in this group. I think if there was one, it would have been the slow demise of her father's and my marriage, and her childhood and teenage feelings of abandonment by both of us. However, an update to Giana's treatment plan made on September 20 clarifies her inclusion in Seeking Safety: "Giana has struggled with symptoms of anxiety in the past . . . She will practice application of healthy coping skills to manage problematic thoughts, feelings, and behaviors." So apparently this group was being used to "treat" Giana's anxiety.

Each chapter of Seeking Safety is introduced by a quotation, usually from a writer or a philosopher. The quotes chosen are instructive. The chapter "Recovery Thinking" is prefaced by a quote from the children's classic *The Little Engine That Could* by Watty Piper, a book I read to all my children. The quote is "I think I can, I think I can, I think I can." This is the mantra that the little train engine repeated to itself when confronted with doing something daunting, like pulling a heavy load up an enormous hill. The message? It must be that if you think strongly enough that you can beat addiction, then you will be able to do that. In Step One a person is powerless over the substance, but if you think hard enough that you can, you will become powerful enough to gain control over it?

One also has to ponder how this squares with the concept of addiction as a disease, a chronic disease requiring continual care and characterized by relapse, among other things. I have tried to understand this by comparing it to treatment for other chronic diseases that require continual care, without which the patient is in increased danger, like my hypertension. When I was first diagnosed with hypertension, which runs in my family, my doctor wanted to put me on medication, but I wanted to try to control it by "lifestyle changes"—that is, I wanted to cure my hypertension through "thinking I can" and then behaving that way. I was already exercising three times a week, but I increased it to five or six times a week. My doctor recommended that I lose twenty pounds, but I was only able to lose ten, despite a very healthy, low-fat, low-salt, plant-based diet. I kept track of calories and was eating the correct amount. When I tried to dip under that, I was hungry all the time. I don't smoke, but I do drink wine. I cut down on that. Six months later, I returned to the doctor. Uh-oh. My blood pressure was lower but still too high. Did the doctor tell me that I had not thought "I think I can" hard enough? No, he told me that I was doing a great job, but I needed to take medication. The risk was still there, especially if I "relapsed" by gaining weight, or drinking more, and as hypertension often has a genetic component, like addiction, I might not be able to control it with behavioral and thought process changes alone. And in both cases, hypertension and OUD, the consequence of not receiving medication increases the likelihood of fatality.

According to the notes, Giana attended three Seeking Safety sessions during her time at Caron; the first on October 1, then on October 15, and the final one on December 3. All were facilitated by addiction counselors. Six to eight of the twenty-five topics in the curriculum appear to have been covered. Some of the exercises in the chapter "Recovery Thinking" encourage practicing what is often called "positive self-talk." So, the materials suggest, instead of saying, "I have no self-discipline," say, "I can learn self-discipline."

I agree that self-discipline can be learned, at least to some extent. Giana was a hugely self-disciplined person in certain ways. What does it take to swim eighty thousand yards a week, getting up for practice at 4:30 a.m. and going back to the pool at 4:00 p.m. and then doing homework afterward and getting excellent grades? What does it take to successfully undertake a science curriculum that included organic chemistry and various courses in anatomy, pharmacology, and physiology while working and when you had been an undergrad English major? Self-discipline, among other characteristics, certainly.

But isn't part of the definition of the disease of addiction that you are *unable to change the behavior even when you are aware of and experiencing the negative consequences?* And if somehow Giana could have *learned* a new type of self-discipline that would have led to conquering her addiction, how long would that have taken? Was there time to do it before she died of the disease?

Chapter Fifteen

Childhood memories are fidgety, unreliable things. You are sure that you have a clear picture of that Thanksgiving when everyone was snowed in, and then your mother tells you that, in fact, the snow ended shortly after dinner and we all went home on slippery roads. Those early memories are sometimes things suggested by pictures we have seen or stories we've been told. We actually don't have a firsthand memory of them at all.

I have a memory of which there are no pictures. I spoke of it to my mother over the years, and she fleshed it out for me. In my memory my mother dressed me in church clothes, fancy occasion clothes. A dress, white socks, and white gloves, a hat for sure. We were going to take the train downtown! Every time we did that, I got to see the big bronze eagle in Wanamaker's, a legendary department store across from the train station. Usually when that happened it was Christmas, and we would stroll past the stores on Market Street for as long as we could stand the cold and take in the lavishly decorated windows with their mobile tableaus. So exciting! It was 1957.

But we weren't going shopping. My mother packed a small overnight bag for us. I don't remember how we got to the station; it wasn't within walking distance of our house. We only had one car, and my father used it most of the time. When we got off the train, my mother hailed a cab, a new experience. I had perhaps been in one before but didn't remember it. In the cab my mother told me we were going to visit my aunt. Even my six-year-old reasoning told me that this was odd. Generally my mother would have prepared me for such a visit. And since my aunt had only one bed, I couldn't understand how we would spend the night.

My aunt, who at times seemed elderly and stern and at other times quite cosmopolitan, had a penchant for fancy hats. She was what in those days was called, in whispers, a spinster, or worse, an old maid. She had a job, lived alone in a large studio apartment on the twentieth floor, with a bellman and an elevator operator, all of which I thought was quite marvelous. I can picture her apartment easily: chintz pillows, ceramic statues, and quite a few books.

We were there to run away from my father, who had been drinking heavily and had apparently not come home the night before. This was not explained to me at the time, but I do remember hearing some adult saying that when he did come home and found us gone, he walked up and down the street, asking the neighbors if they knew where we were. The resolution came when my aunt, his older sister, called him and worked out a truce. Whatever promises he made, they didn't include stopping drinking or getting help, or if they did, he broke those promises. A decade later he died of alcoholism.

I can recall my mother and grandmother warning us that alcoholism "runs in families" and we should always be on guard. Indeed. The Surgeon General's report states that "genetic factors are thought to account for 40 to 70 percent of the individual differences in risk for addiction" (2–22). Giana had genetic risk factors for addiction and mental illness all over the place. In addition to my father's alcoholism, I am told by an older family member on his side that his mother had problems with severe anxiety and drank to self-medicate. She died at forty-four. His father was also a heavy drinker who also died before I was born. My mother and I have both been medicated and treated for depression and anxiety. My maternal grandfather had a compulsive gambling addiction that ruined his marriage and his career.

My maternal great-grandparents both had "nervous breakdowns," as they were called then, and there was alcoholism resulting in early death in that generation. One of my brothers is an alcoholic. On Giana's father's side, there was history of mental illness and drug use by one uncle, and another died in a car accident while drunk.

In several of Giana's rehab experiences, there were discussions, family tree exercises, and even worksheet activities about "generational addiction." These exercises, however, were about learned behaviors, not about genes. Unlike diseases such as Tay-Sachs or sickle cell or the genetic mutations in the breast cancer genes BRCA 1 and 2, in 12-Step–based programs "treating" substance use disorder, the focus is on the character defects and aberrant behavior of the patient.

~

My mother was meant for a life she did not get. She wanted a life where she could plant and tend a "kitchen garden" like the one she helped with as a child, where the vegetables and herbs used by the family were grown right out the back door. She wanted a large flower garden and fresh flowers in the house every day. She wanted to raise a lot of children, bake peach pies, and tend house. She wanted to volunteer. She wanted a kind husband who could generally be relied upon, like the grandfather she grew up with and not like her father, who left the family when she was five.

When that happened, my grandmother parked my mother with her genteel Southern parents, both school teachers, and went off to Columbia to get a master's degree. She never remarried and supported herself quite well, visiting my mother regularly and sending money for her care. Unlike the other women in her family, my mother had little interest in academics, wasn't ambitious, and didn't have any desire for a career. While my grandmother was reading political biographies and I was reading fiction, my mother was reading *Bon Appetit* and *Better Homes and Gardens*. She was stunningly beautiful, stylish, sweet-tempered, and passive. Her judgment and common sense were frequently questionable. Nowhere was that more evident than in her initial intense attraction to my father and her marriage at age twenty.

Instead of what she wanted, she got a handsome alcoholic husband with a scary temper whose progressive disease made it impossible for him to work after I was about nine or ten. She kept on trying to create her dream life long past when it was remotely possible until finally, in a fruitless attempt to keep our house, she ended up with a part-time job as a cashier in a used car lot because she had never gone to college or pursued a career. While occasionally at midday she hollered at my father to get out of bed, she generally avoided him. By the time I was eleven or twelve, she was sleeping in my room. I would wake up in the middle of the night to find her doing laundry or vacuuming somewhere in the house, my father passed out or not home. For a long while, she went to great lengths to protect the veneer of a lovely home and family, until finally it became necessary to move in with my grandmother, by then retired, who put an addition on her house.

While she avoided my father, I did not. I was only a little bit afraid of him and didn't have much trouble defending my younger siblings and telling him, profanity and all, what I thought about him. Usually I was able to outrun him or wiggle past him, but when I couldn't, he struck hard. My relationship with him was nonexistent except for these confrontations. With my mother consumed by trying to hold things together with her low-paying job and the younger kids, I did whatever I wanted. Some of that wasn't entirely terrible; while I cut school a lot, I spent most of that free time reading, usually at a library if it was too cold to be outside. I had a job at a toy store, where I had lied about my age. I ended up hanging out in the coffeehouses of the day, listening to folk music and meeting guys who were way too old for me.

When my mother left to go to my grandmother's, I didn't join her but quit school and started living on my own. I detested high school. My grandmother wasn't happy with what I was doing, and my mother was too depressed to pay much attention. They had their hands full with making ends meet and taking care of my siblings. I lived with friends, traveled to California, worked as a waitress and a retail clerk. In various ways I worked against the war in Vietnam for five years—marching, organizing, writing, and helping to raise money and manage an office for the work to take place. I read my way through Tolstoy and Dostoyevsky before turning to Thomas Mann, Virginia Woolf, Fitzgerald, Hemingway, Faulkner, and and then to James Baldwin Somehow I got interested in astronomy and started reading about that. I liked painting and went to art museums. I had numerous boyfriends. Some years later, when I decided I wanted to go to college, I took a GED test and passed everything, and then went on to college and graduate school, both of which I loved. My interest in education as a college major was partially sparked by my experience—I couldn't figure out exactly what I had missed in high school. Dances? Homecoming? Surely there had to be a better way to educate young people. I don't regret anything I did then, but I would have flipped out if any of my kids wanted to drop out of school or travel to California at fifteen. I tell myself it was the sixties, and things were different.

As I got older, one of my aims in life was to *not* be like my mother, and in many ways I succeeded. It took me a long while to realize, however, that the lack of a relationship role model in my grandmother's life, combined with my mother's avoidance and self-effacing demeanor with my father, led me to have no idea what a workable relationship might look like. I had no model of an honest and affectionate give and take with a commitment to joint decision making. The notion that a long-term relationship is based on friendship was unfathomable to me. I never understood how a relationship could begin without a deep fall that required a surrender of self. Then once the self was surrendered, fear followed, and then anger. So as a result, in intimate relationships, I have tended to swing wildly between my grandmother's cool self-sufficiency and my mother's dependency and avoidance of confrontation, her silence.

And maybe that is where Giana perfected her natural inclination to be silent. She was an early talker, stringing together full sentences with clauses before she was two, but she was also very shy and was often quiet around adults until she knew them well. The September she was nineteen months, she started day care at the center where I was the director. I recall her teacher pulling me to the classroom door one day to watch her "reading" from a picture book to a group of dolls and stuffed animals over in a corner. She was quietly telling the story almost verbatim from having heard it a few times. Yet at circle time, she did not talk and sing with the group. She was extremely attached to me. The "handoff" of Giana from me to someone else, be it a teacher, a grandparent, or a babysitter, was always difficult for her, but she didn't cry or yell like my other kids. Instead she tensed her little body and clammed up.

As she got older, when faced with conflict or defeat, she retreated into herself and did not communicate. Unlike my other kids, when she was told she couldn't do something she wanted to do, she went to her room and closed the door. No yelling, no slammed doors. When a race didn't go her way, she didn't explode. She just clenched her teeth and got back in the pool. And when real life intruded into her dreamy romantic relationships with boys and men, she either bolted or quietly demonstrated her considerable passive-aggressive skills.

So back to the term "generational addiction." Never concretely defined for us at the FEP at Caron, it seems to resemble the common ideas about received knowledge, environmental and cultural influences, modeled behavior, and so forth. What wasn't consistently addressed were the implications of this beyond the obvious, something that should have happened in high-quality individual therapy.

Nevertheless, in the notes following a telephone family session, Giana's addiction counselor at Caron made a very insightful point. Talking about Giana's tendency to be quiet to the point of being silent, she observed, "Giana's silence becomes a breeding ground for her dishonesty and manipulation, and thus a place where her disease grows."

~

After my mother's hospital discharge, my siblings and I dealt with the new reality that she would not be able to function safely at home without twenty-four-hour care. We were all working full time. My brother the doctor found a live-in caretaker; I arranged for a hospital bed, an oxygen machine, a wheelchair. The drug treatments were discontinued, but she was still receiving transfusions.

As Thanksgiving approached, she was doing well. She was tired, went to bed earlier than usual, and took a nap each day. But she had shrugged off the oxygen two days after coming home, and she rarely used the wheelchair, preferring a walker. I had set up a baby monitor so she could call for help if she needed to get up in the middle of the night to go to the bathroom. She got up on her own and never asked for help. There was certainly no mental impairment; she read newspapers and magazines as usual, had lively conversations with friends and relatives who called and visited, and liked to participate in cooking.

We arranged for Giana to get a forty-eight-hour pass from

Caron for Thanksgiving. Lou picked her up on Wednesday and brought her to my mother's. I was already there, preparing to cook. My brother T stopped by with a load of firewood and built the first fire of the season. That year Thanksgiving and Hanukkah coincided, and we invited some family members to celebrate on the evening before Thanksgiving. My stepfather was Jewish, as are some other members of my family, so Jewish holidays and traditions were always part of our family life. We couldn't find my stepfather's menorah, so we sent out the call and ended up with three menorahs that evening. Celeste and her kids came over. We made potato latkes, which we supplemented with veggies, and then we sat together in the living room, in the peaceful glow of the fire and menorahs. A little later the children and I made four pumpkin pies while Giana and my mother and the others laughed and talked. Celeste and Giana were both reading the same series of historical fiction, and they discussed those books. I have a video of that evening with a brief glimpse of Giana as she moved from living room to kitchen to help me for a moment. My mother commented to me that while Giana was "present" in everything we did during those two days, she was very quiet.

I recall peeking into my mother's den late that Wednesday night after I had done some preparatory cooking to see Giana curled up on the extra bed, sleeping peacefully. My mother was quiet, asleep in her room. The sweet smell of the pumpkin pies was mingled with the savory scent of sautéed onions and celery, promising a delicious meal and a lovely Thanksgiving. The meal was definitely not as good as it would have been if my mother had been the chief cook, but it was good enough. The next day we sat around the fire long after eating, football games muted on the TV, just talking. Festivities over, I took Giana back to Caron on Friday when the caregiver returned. That was the last time Giana saw my mother.

On the Sunday of Thanksgiving weekend, my brother G

arrived at my mother's from his girlfriend's, where he had spent Thanksgiving. He was going to stay with my mother for a day or two and take her to a doctor's appointment. I was in a meeting Monday morning when G called me to say that Mom was having involuntary twitches. I advised going to the emergency room. He called me back shortly to say she had experienced a major seizure, and an ambulance was coming. I flew out of work and met him at the hospital. Shortly after I got there, my mother had another seizure, terrifying to watch. Her face turned purple, and she gritted her teeth so tightly I thought they would crack. Eventually she was admitted to intensive care. That was December 1.

Meanwhile, Giana's discharge date had been set as December 12, my mother's birthday. When her discharge planning began at Caron, the idea was for Giana to move to a structured recovery setting, but with a routine that gave her more freedom to begin establishing her independence. For the most part, we relied on Caron to choose an appropriate aftercare setting for Giana. No one thought it was a good idea for Giana to be in Philadelphia, where associations with drug use were rife and where it would be easy for her to resume old habits and connections. Initially, Caron staff gave her the names of a few places to check out. I remember that one was a facility that included daily equine care as part of its program. That sounded good to me—she could use her veterinary skills. But when she called, it appeared that the program was very similar to Caron's and offered no avenue to more independence, so it was scratched from the list.

Somewhere in this search Giana expressed the possibility of going to Colorado, because if it wasn't wise to be in the Philadelphia area, at least she could be near Louisa. I think both

Caron and Giana did research into possibilities in Colorado. After checking out various options, the one that seemed the most suitable was The Rose House. This facility had a small residential program in addition to several "step-down" houses, where patients who had been sober at least three months lived together in small groups. They were to attend one group a week at the primary facility, one a week at the house, therapy once a week, and random drug testing. Giana's counselor was supposed to ensure that she find a job, get a sponsor, and attend daily NA meetings. In addition, Giana would receive services from a consulting psychiatrist. Caron looked into it and approved; someone from the clinical staff had been at a conference with the founder of The Rose House and felt comfortable with her. We relied upon Caron's judgment about the suitability and quality of the facility.

Still, Giana was ambivalent about going to Colorado. On the one hand, she knew very well the mantra against being around familiar "people, places, and things" that might act as triggers. Also, she said she was bored with the same treatment routine at Caron and ready for something different. But truly, she just wanted to come home to my house. Giana expressed repeatedly, with sorrow and dismay, that she had no home, which was essentially true: she had given up her apartment over a year earlier, our family home had been sold, and after she entered Eagleville, I had told her that she had to have a minimum of six months sober before staying with me. At the point she left for Colorado, it was five months. "Having no home" had become a trope for not having a place she felt secure, both physically and psychologically, a place where she could care for her beloved dog, a place where she felt useful and efficacious. "Homeless" was a symbol of everything she had lost.

What if I had just let her come home? Could the outcome have been any worse? Might it have been better?

When my mother "woke up" after the seizures, she seemed

to have lost most mental functioning. She wasn't talking, wasn't making eye contact, didn't even open her mouth to accept food. Tests were done. Then suddenly, two days later, she was sitting up and laughing and speaking. When her hematologist entered the room, he was very surprised when she greeted him with a smile and a warm "Hello!" I have a video of myself telling her that there had been a severe cold spell in Colorado and that people were ice skating on the lake near Louisa's house. She responds with "Really? You're kidding!" and laughs. She seemed very comfortable with all of us but couldn't name any of us. Then that night, as quickly as she had "woken up," she lapsed into sleep and didn't wake up. Where did that brief return to language and the conventions of conversation come from? When there was no subsequent return to consciousness, the doctors told us that further treatment would not be useful. The next day, December 5, we made the decision to transfer her to a hospice facility. I remember sitting in the hospital room with my sister, waiting for the ambulance that would take her there. All the machines had been turned off, and my mother was sleeping peacefully. It was very quiet, and there was nothing to say.

Meanwhile, I was extremely concerned about Giana's depression and, in the week before her discharge, asked her addiction counselor over the phone whether discharge at this point was a good idea. My mother was in hospice, clearly dying, and Giana had verbalized being sad about it to me and, as I found later in the Caron notes, to them. I thought the discharge should be delayed. I was assured that Giana was ready and mostly wanted to go. So I let it happen. As an additional support, we also enrolled Giana in Caron's "My First Year," an eight-thousand-dollar follow-up service that included calls from staff at Caron, online support groups, and more random drug testing (Giana would be directed to get a drug test at a lab), among other features. I would like to believe that if I had not been so consumed with my mother, I would have been more involved in the choice of facility and indeed in Giana's discharge. I don't know if that is true, but no amount of "positive self-talk" or assurances from my therapist and family will convince me that I did the best I could do at the time for my daughter.

What were we thinking? We knew my mother was about to die. What if I had followed my gut, at least said, "Not until after my mother passes and we have time to mourn as a family."

The plan was for Caron to take Giana to the airport on December 12, and she would fly to Colorado to enter The Rose House. On Sunday December 8, I went to Caron to visit Giana for the last time before her discharge to The Rose House. I was worried about leaving hospice—what if my mother died while I was gone?—but I felt I had to see Giana before she left. If I didn't take her dog, Jade, to Caron, who knew when Giana would see her again? My sisters, always generous, urged me to go. I was going to spend four hours or so with her, taking the dog to a nearby park where we had played before. But soon after I arrived, it began to snow, lightly at first, but it was very windy and cold. We played for a little while at an outdoor area on the Caron grounds, and then when the weather worsened, we sat in my car. After about two hours we decided I'd better go, but I was very reluctant. I didn't want Giana to leave Caron. I might have tried to pay them forever just to have those Sunday visits with her. Giana went to her residence and brought back several bags of clothing, books, journals and notes, and other stuff that she didn't plan to take to Colorado. The journal and notes are here in my study. The rest is still in bins in my basement. She called me from a Caron phone a few minutes after I had left to warn me that the turnpike was closed as the result of an icy pileup. I remember her greeting on the phone: "Mom, it's me."

Every day I long to hear that greeting again.

Giana left Caron fragile and unwell. Three days before her discharge, she shared in her daily addiction counseling group that she was very sad about my mother's dire prognosis. The counselor writes: "Giana appeared attentive but in despair during the session. She was tearful throughout the session and struggled to view her emotional state as anything but 'depression.'"The day before her discharge, in a Family of Origin group, Giana read a letter she had written as her present self to the person she was when she arrived at Caron four months earlier. The addiction counselor's note states, "She was tearful when reading the letter and remains in a place of fear and sadness around the completion of treatment." Fear and sadness? Yes, and she'd been communicating that for months. As she expresses so often in her Tenth-Step inventories, and as is everywhere in the notes, she was fearful about her ability to remain abstinent. She was fearful because of the state of her mental health. She was sad about all her losses, sad about what she viewed as her failure in treatment, sad about her loneliness.

Giana's discharge summary states the following: "Giana remains at high risk for relapse due to her history of relapse after short amounts of sobriety and disclosure around her increase in negative body image and thoughts about participating in romantic relationships that she has identified as unhealthy for her." When I read this now, I am disgusted and enraged. Knowing the increased risk of lethality when relapse occurs after a period of abstinence, why did they discharge her, especially without strong urging for her to take Vivitrol? They had releases for Lou and me. Why did they not talk about this frightening prognosis?

After an early flight, Giana arrived at The Rose House on the morning of December 12. Lou, who was working in Colorado at the time, came to see her and visited where she would be living.

He shopped with her for necessities, had her phone reactivated, and opened a bank account that Louisa would control.

My mother died the following morning. When I called Giana to let her know, there was silence, followed by a quiet bleat, like a wounded animal. Giana's initial clinical assessment was completed that day. In answer to a question about having experienced the death of a close family member, she wrote: "My grandmother—we were very close—and she was supportive. She died today, 12/13/13. I am very sad."

Giana's maternal grandmother feeding her, 1980

Chapter Sixteen

So began the last three weeks of Giana's life.

In a document dated December 13, 2013, and titled "Rose House Residential Treatment Plan," under a section titled "Current Psychiatric Status," the writer lists depressed mood and anxiety and characterizes both as "severe." The "Plan of Action" for this is described: Individual therapy once a week for one hour, house meeting once a week, relapse prevention once a week, five 12-Step meetings per week.

This "psychiatric status" report had not been conducted by a psychiatrist or even a doctor but by the therapist who was doing the intake on Giana. There was, however, a psychiatrist involved with Giana. Within a few days of her arrival, the psychiatrist, who was a contractor with The Rose House, changed Giana's medication, from Cymbalta back to Paxil. I have no notes from this psychiatrist named Charles Park; when I sent a certified request for Giana's records, it came back indicating the postal service was unable to get his signature. The Rose House told me that they had no records by him about Giana because he was a contractor, not an employee.

On December 18, Giana's therapist at The Rose House conducted the first therapy session and wrote the following:

"Giana's affect was flat with hunched posture and downward gaze, and verbal tone was flat and soft. She appeared apathetic and unmotivated. She expressed feeling this way also, giving the example that all she wants to do right now is sleep and not get out of bed. We considered possible strategies to curb the depressive symptoms she is experiencing and decided on her continuing to address each of her tasks for recovery and attaining employment, regardless of internal motivation or feeling, and that in time hopefully the medication changes will begin to have a positive effect. If she is still feeling this way in two weeks she will be required to come to the Rose House [meaning the main building] twice a week for DBT."

Giana had been treated with dialectical behavior therapy or therapy that was supposed to be DBT at other locations, most recently Caron. As in the past, an intervention that had failed previously several times was again recommended. That she had previously been treated with DBT is noted on her intake form.

Here is what I knew about The Rose House then. The Rose House was (and is) a residential treatment facility for women that, in addition to its primary inpatient program, included three "step-down" units, sober living houses that were open to women who had been sober for a minimum of three months (Giana had been sober for five months). Giana's house had four women, including her. There was no staff member living there, although supposedly there was continuous check-in from Rose House staff. Weekly, Giana was supposed to be participating in daily 12-Step meetings, one counseling group at the primary facility, one group at her house, and one individual counseling session, and she would receive services from a psychiatrist with whom The Rose House contracted, at an additional cost. Her counselor was supposed to ensure that she find a job, get a sponsor, and attend NA meetings. The Rose House was to conduct random drug testing. Louisa visited the house where Giana would live; of course, she had no basis on which to make a professional judgment but found that it was well maintained and the staff member who met her there was friendly and accessible. However, we relied upon Caron's judgment about the suitability and safety of the facility. Louisa, after all, was a teacher, with no professional medical or psychological training.

What I didn't know about The Rose House then, but found out later, is that at the time of Giana's stay there, it was unlicensed.

During the next ten days, Giana went to NA meetings daily and spent time with Louisa and her husband, although of course both of them were working. She and I communicated by text and phone. She was looking for jobs online. Louisa says that she vacillated between depression and irritability. She was very annoyed that she had to get two sets of drug tests, one for Caron's My First Year and one for The Rose House, and that she had to travel some distance by public transportation to do this. I realize now that she must have been at home alone quite often during the day, as her roommates were working.

Giana's next therapy appointment was scheduled for December 26, but on that day she was flying to Philadelphia. We had decided to have a memorial gathering for my mother the weekend after Christmas. Giana flew in with Louisa and her husband two days prior to the service. Giana had experienced a recurrence of her back injury and hobbled out of the airport looking gaunt and depressed. I was alarmed, but Louisa was just annoyed—her husband has ongoing back problems, and her view was that Giana always received undue attention to her ailments, encouraging her victim mentality. In addition, Giana had been inaccessible and negative with them, and they were understandably frustrated. We all should have taken that as a sign that her recovery was in danger and the current plan wasn't working. I think we were all conveying to Giana that it was time for her to "buck up." In retrospect, the possibility of that time had been lost long before.

From the airport we went out to lunch, and a perplexing incident ensued. I left the restaurant for a few minutes to go to a nearby store and pick up a few items. Giana texted me and told me to buy a drug test kit because she thought that Louisa and her husband suspected she was using. She wanted to take a drug test to prove that she wasn't. I didn't buy the kit, and when I returned to the restaurant, I raised the issue. Louisa and her husband denied thinking that, and in the interest of peacefulness and keeping the focus on my mother, I smoothed it over and we went on with our lunch.

What if I had forced a discussion? What if she was already far along the relapse road and her paranoia about what they thought was the result of her own semi-formed plans to use?

After lunch we decided to go to my house to exchange Christmas presents and see her dog, Jade. The last time she had seen Jade was the last time I'd visited her at Caron, a few weeks earlier. We sat in my living room, the scent of the large Douglas fir filling the downstairs. In the adjoining dining room, on the windows, were the curtains that Giana and I had picked out over a year earlier for the bedroom she was planning to occupy in our former family home. I remember being in the store and swirling among all the curtain samples as if we were doing a ritual dance. Her recurring relapses prevented her from staying in that house, which was sold. The curtains, never hung, were stored in a closet in my house, until one of my dining room curtains got stained, and I used the ones meant for her bedroom as a replacement. I cringe now thinking about how she must have felt when she saw them—another reminder of the life she had derailed. I had only a stuffed stocking for her and told her that we would go shopping for clothes when I came to Colorado to visit in February. She deflected me, embarrassed at the meager gifts she had for me and thinking, I surmise, that she didn't feel entitled to gifts. It was a joyless exchange.

My mother's memorial service was at my brother's house, two days later. It was a balmy day, ridiculously warm for the 28th of December. Relatives and friends filled the house, still decorated for Christmas, and spilled out to the deck. I have several pictures of Giana standing on the deck, hand in hand with my sister. My last pictures of her are from that day, and one more taken that evening by Dina as she lay in our house on the sofa with Jade.

My brother and my son-in-law had put together a slideshow of pictures of my mother and the family that looped on his huge TV; there were pictures of her displayed everywhere. Giana's back had improved, and she had made an effort to present herself well: she wore a long black skirt and a black-and-gray top. I was busy throughout the day, setting up food and drink, greeting people, and planning for my remarks when the formal memorial began. As I moved about the big house, I saw Giana, circulating and talking to people. I believe that was a hard day for her; in addition to being sad about my mother, it was difficult seeing her many cousins, family friends, and even a few of her old friends. We had not been very public about her struggles, but everyone knew she had not been well, and for her to chat with this old friend who had recently graduated from law school and had a baby, and this cousin who was in graduate school, and this one whose third baby was on her hip . . . she must have been haunted about what she had lost in her own life.

We never got a chance to talk about it, though. Giana and her sister and brother-in-law were leaving at dawn the next morning, a Sunday, to return to Colorado. They left my brother's in the early evening to go back to my house, pack, and get some rest. I stayed until the last guest was gone and helped clean up. By the time I got home, they were sleeping, Louisa and her husband in the guest room. Giana was in my bed, curled up and asleep. I whispered a goodnight. In the early morning, still dark, we bolted from bed and drove to the airport. I gave them all a quick hug and they were gone.

It was the last time I saw Giana.

What if I had put my arms around you the morning you were supposed to leave and we had drifted in sleep until we woke again, together?

After they left, I was extremely worried about Giana's depression. She had tried to reach Dr. Park, but he was on vacation, and no substitute was provided. On January 1 I sent this email to her Rose House therapist:

Hi [. . .], this is Giana's mother, Elise Schiller. I'm writing because I'm concerned about Giana. First, she seems quite depressed. I know that the psychiatrist is in the process of switching her meds. She's back on Paxil, which has worked well for her in the past, but currently she's at a relatively low dose. I think Giana contacted you to ask about seeing the psychiatrist (I don't know his name)—I hope that will happen within the next few days.

Also, I think Giana needs more than once a week therapy. Is there a way for her to see you or the psychiatrist more frequently? She has insurance, and her father and I have the ability to pay if necessary.

The next day, January 2, the therapist called me to tell me that he had seen her and that he felt she was doing better. She was attending daily NA meetings, and he was pressuring her about getting a sponsor.

That evening it started to snow in Philadelphia, with a large accumulation predicted. I exchanged texts with Giana that night, at about ten o'clock. I said: "Snowing like mad here. Everything will be shut down tomorrow." Giana responded: "Ugh, but probably pretty." I wrote back: "Very pretty. They've already closed the schools."

The next morning, with almost a foot of snow on the ground and the city declaring a snow emergency, I closed our offices. I texted Giana at 9:47 a.m. Philadelphia time and said: "I took Jade out and let her off the leash and she ran—or jumped like a deer—back and forth between my house and next door." Giana replied: "I love when she does that." A few hours later I sent her a picture of the backyard and said: "It's very cold. Jade had to wear her jacket. What are you doing today?"

She replied that she and Louisa were going to meet at Louisa's vet, where Giana was going to apply for a job. Louisa had an appointment for her cat. They were also going to do some other errands and go out to lunch. We texted back and forth during the day. I cut up some vegetables, browned some meat, and combined it all in the Crock-Pot to stew slowly. I thought about my mother, as I often did (and do) when cooking. We had only begun to dismantle her apartment, starting first with the fridge, freezer, and pantry. I thought about the large apartment without her in it, but with most of the rooms completely intact, every painting, picture, book, knickknack, and piece of furniture where she had last seen it. I walked through the rooms in a mental tour. I had a fierce urge to drive there and come through the door as I had countless times to the smell of fresh flowers, the voice of Tony Bennett, and her offer of tea and cookies.

I spent several hours that afternoon on the phone with our chief financial officer, reviewing the status of various grants and general expenditures, both of us snowbound but determined to get the work done that we had planned to do in the office. I took Jade out again in the late afternoon as the gray light waned. We played in the snow in a nearby churchyard. It was beautiful and peaceful. Apart from the heavy snowfall, it was just a regular day.

I poured a glass of wine and sat in the glow of the Christmas tree for a while before going to bed, about eleven.

January 3:

letter written to Giana by Louisa on January 3, anniversary of Giana's death. It was sent to family d posted on a website for those who have lost someone to … ance use disorder.)

Today I write to you beautiful Giana, my little sister. How can it be a year without you when I feel the details of the day 1.3.14 are so vivid? It is not hard, details don't fade, the day was so normal, so very blasé. For some reason it is important for me to recollect the day here since it was our day. S and I were the only ones to spend it with you. You made it an important day. I won't go into what I know now that changes the day, I'll just remember it the way it was. It was an unusually warm day, a little windy, a little sunny but not bright blue skies. We both had our jackets but didn't need them. We had a plan to meet at my Vet bright and early (8:00 or 8:30 a.m.) where I had an appointment for the cat and I had gotten you a job interview (you got the job). You were late from the bus because you took the bus the wrong way. You called me and I looked out the window of the vet to make sure you were walking the right way. You walked down South Broadway in your North Face jacket. When you got to the vet, you had a red folder with your resume. You didn't sit down, you paced a little. I thought you were nervous for the interview. You were wearing a pale blue shirt (blue is your favorite color) and jeans. I think you wore gray UGG boots but it could have been your nicer brown boots. Your hair was long, long, long and beautiful as always. You had some make-up on. I wore dark blue jeans and a white shirt and ballet flats. They took you for a tour and I waited on you. We left the cat there. Then we got in my car and drove it to the dealer because the heating vent was acting up. We left it there and walked down the creek path a little bit to Barnes and Noble. You had a Starbucks card and tried to use it for coffee but they said no. We sat in the café and I read Divergent and you got some magazines. Matthew McConaughey was on the cover of one and you wanted to show me how different he looked with his weight loss for the movie Dallas Buyers Club. We sat there for a while. They called and said the car was ready but S called and said he wanted to have lunch with us. We walked to the mall and went to California Pizza Kitchen. You sat across from S and me in a booth. We ordered salads and ice tea and lemonade for me. You had a chicken Caesar salad. We talked about the weather as a storm was coming. We talked about Mom and your dog Jade as there was already a storm in Philly and Mom had sent you pictures of Jade playing in the snow. We talked about going to the movies the next day. We talked about seizing the day as someone at S's work was diagnosed with cancer. We talked about sobriety and how it means being sober of ALL things. You said that. We talked about people who were with you at your rehab and how some of them were semi-famous.

We wanted you to come home with me and go to a meeting in Longmont. S asked you to come over and run around the lake with him as he was starting his running plan. You said I could never run around the lake. He said you could, and he was pressing the issue because he really wanted to share that with you. (In the year since you have become his running partner anyway.) I said you could walk with me instead? You made an excuse that you were going to go to a meeting at 5:30 around your house and get a ride back from the old timer. We talked about you continuing to look for sponsors. We walked S back to his office and walked back to get the car. You said you had the hiccups and didn't feel great. You still had a phlegmy cough. You looked a little pale. We got the car and drove back to the vet to pick up the cat. You stayed in the car and helped me put her in the back seat. Then we were going to drive you back to your house. I insisted we stop at Walgreens for Mucinex for you. I waited in the car and gave you the credit card we were using for expenses. You got Mucinex and some tootsie rolls. You gave me the card back. We drove to your house. We didn't talk about anything that specific. I pulled into your driveway. You said thank you for the vet hookup. I said, of course, I'm glad it will work out. We made plans to look at the movies and the weather. I said let me know how your meeting went or something like that.

I didn't say I love you but I usually did. I said it on the phone the day before so you knew how much I loved you. I watched you walk up, your hair shone in the sun. There was a large box on your front stoop. You grabbed it with one arm and put it under your armpit. Then you went inside and that was the last time I or anyone to my knowledge saw you alive. You weren't trying too hard to get away from me although you had heroin in your room. I have turned back the clock in my head so many times, I have tried to think of throwing the car in park and running up to you on the front stoop and holding you and hugging you and asking you to come with me. I have thought about at least going inside. I didn't check your room, I didn't know I should. I went home, I talked to Mom, I took a bike ride around the lake, I took a nap. I made dinner for S and me. I texted you—how was your meeting? Any sponsorship possibilities? You didn't text back. S went to his group, and I watched TV. He came home and we watched Dexter. I was wearing pink PJ bottoms with cats on them, and a gray hoodie. I fell asleep on the chair I used to sit in. The phone rang around 10:50 or later and it was Mom. I missed it. It rang again —I said to S, uh-oh, I texted Giana earlier and got no response and now my mom is calling me. I was thinking you got caught using or called her to admit to using. I picked it up and heard the news. It was the most gut wrenching, punch in the stomach, traumatic moment of my life. We flew into action but there was nothing we could do at the moment. I talked to all kinds of people, S did EVERYTHING, then I said I needed to get out of the house and we went to Perkins and I drank hot cocoa with whipped cream and stared at all the people there who had no idea my sister was dead. I didn't sleep at all. It snowed and snowed and I thought that was the first sign from you—you LOVED winter and snow. That was the whole day, the whole last day of your life. I am thankful I had it with you.

~

People were coming and going all that week. It was as if I had suddenly contracted multiple personality disorder. The social self that has learned the drill does what is necessary. *Thanks for the food. Yes, please come back tomorrow. Have you called X and Y? I'm going to take a shower.* And then part of the time you are vacant. I remember going into my therapist's office but nothing about who was with me or what was said. Maybe I just cried. A memorial was being planned for the coming weekend at the park where Giana had spent a lot of time with her dogs. I have no memory of how that decision was made. I recall going with Lou to inquire about a place to hold a meal and gathering afterward, but that's not the place we eventually went, and I don't remember any of the planning for the place where we did go. Pieces of the experience go missing.

Another part of you is in complete denial. It was many months before the concrete thought "she is dead" was not immediately followed by the suggestion "but maybe she isn't." From the vantage point of four years, I examine my behavior then and I see how many things I did that indicated I didn't fully believe in her death. Within a few days, I took possession of my phone. For a long time, at least half a year, whenever a call or text came in and I wasn't wearing my glasses and could not clearly see the name on the screen, I felt hopeful it might be her. Calling me from where? How? Those logical questions did not immediately arise. I did not remove her contact information from my phone for two years, although I avoided the section where it was stored. Months after Giana's death, with reality sinking in, I had to ask a coworker to please change her cathedral bells ringtone.

Now I know the reason I insisted there be no obituary is that I thought if it appeared in the paper, it might be true.

I also insisted that there be no cemetery, no burial. It was impossible for me to imagine a burial. I couldn't breathe at the thought of Giana, her lanky body that I knew so well, confined in a box under the ground. Sometime during that week, my beautiful daughter's body was torn apart by an autopsy and then cremated in Colorado. Maybe I thought about it that week, but I don't remember. I have thought about it a lot since. What day did it happen? What time? What was I doing? Was she naked when she was cremated? One day a few years ago, I opened the autopsy report and began to read. I only got through a few sentences before putting it down, and I've never looked at it again. Louisa and her husband made the arrangements, with financial help from Lou. They left me out of it. The only thing I remember saying, perhaps to my son-in-law, was that I wanted her hair. Her very long, thick, wavy, deep brown hair.

Louisa and her husband arrived in Philadelphia with the ashes, a box from the funeral home containing her hair, and a package from the coroner's office. All of that was put in hiding, away from me. I didn't see any of it until much later. There were miniature urns of ashes for the family, which we used when we had a memorial service in the park, eight days after she died. I don't think I saw them until that morning, but I might be wrong.

The morning of the service was eerily warm, and there were still patches of the previous week's snow on the ground. We stood in a big circle on a hill above the pond where Abby used to jump and swim. Mist rose from everywhere. My nephew took pictures of the pond with the mist rising and put them on Facebook.

It only occurred to me briefly not to say something at the service, because I felt that I might not be able to get through it. I decided that if I was unable to continue once I'd started, people would understand. At first I thought about reading a poem; of the few that came to mind, Lou actually read one of them, "To an Athlete Dying Young." Instead, I decided to read one that Giana had written as a child, a happy poem, and to talk a little about her. I brought a huge, blown-up picture of her as a seven-year-old, taken on the deck of my grandmother's beach house. My brother-in-law, Uncle D, was crying.

What's all this?

I can't remember if anyone else spoke.

As we stood in that big circle, a large black dog wandered lazily in, casually greeting various people. It's a sign, several people murmured. I have been an agnostic, not a believer or disbeliever, all of my life. I accept that there are mysteries, but I doubt that divinity can explain them. And yet . . .

> There are more things in heaven and earth, Horatio,
> Than are dreamt of in your philosophy (I, v 166–167).

Says Hamlet.

Afterward we went to a restaurant a block away. A buffet had been set up. I don't know who selected the food, maybe it was me. It was only family, but there were a lot of us. My son had made a video montage. I kept wandering out of the main room, away from the noise, the video, the people, and the food I couldn't eat.

On the way home from the restaurant, I insisted to James that we go to a pet store to buy Jade a raincoat. I recall feeling a great urgency about it. He started to turn the car in that direction, and then he looked at me and firmly said no. He took me home and guided me to my bed. There were people downstairs, talking, drinking tea or wine, I have no idea. After a while I came downstairs and sat. I remember my brother and his girlfriend were there. She had lost a brother to heroin, but that was not being discussed. The small talk designed not to upset me went on.

Sometime that week, I received a call from the director of The Rose House, a woman who had lost her daughter to drugs. After offering condolences, her advice to me was to look for "signs." She said her daughter had left her signs, including placing a certain book of poetry in an unusual place where it wouldn't normally be. I had no idea how to respond to her and never spoke to her again.

So it was that, despite dismissing the talk of signs to the many people who encouraged me to look for them, I left a small dog charm that had broken off one of Giana's bracelets on my window sill. I waited for it to move, to disappear, to reappear somewhere else. One night I woke suddenly, panicked that it was not there, but upon checking, it was exactly where I'd left it. It's still there, only moved when I dust.

I also received a call from one of the spiritual staff at Caron. He consoled me by saying, "We all knew that Giana was very addicted." That snapped me back to some level of reality. I contentiously replied that if they had thought that, why had they discharged her?

That day I suddenly got very angry. I looked around my house at the cards and the flowers and the pictures of Giana bracketed with candles. *God damn you! How could you cause all of us so much pain? Always self-involved! Always self-centered! Always needing more than you gave!* I emptied the vases and threw the flowers in the trash. I swept up all the pictures and put them in a bin in the basement and then went through the house removing every picture of her, took down her framed diplomas, and collected her art work from over the years that decorated various bookshelves. I removed from the wall the tiny ceramic handprint that she had made me in kindergarten. Everything I could find—books, CDs, jewelry, cosmetics, shoes—anything that was hers went into the farthest, darkest corner in the basement.

Giana and her brother, Greg, circa 2005

Chapter Seventeen

Two thousand fourteen. It was a year of births and deaths, starting with yours, my sweet girl. It was a year of reckoning, of trying to understand how to be in the world without you and my mother.

One strategy was to do things differently than in the past. I had tickets to visit you and Louisa in February. You and I had talked a few times about how, when I came in February, we would go shopping and take a ride up to Rocky Mountain National Park, one of our favorite places in winter. We'd go sledding. When February came, there was a fortuitous snowstorm in Philly, my flight was canceled, and when I thought of rescheduling the trip, I realized that I didn't want to be in Colorado. You weren't there to go sledding and shopping. Rather abruptly, Louisa and I decided to go to a resort hotel in Arizona. Not the Grand Canyon, where I'd been with you several times, but just a hotel with an enormous pool outside of Phoenix. There was a casino nearby that we didn't go to. Mostly I sat at the pool, reading and staring at giant cacti. I floated in the water for hours, all my previous zeal for exercise gone.

Unexpectedly, about ten weeks after you died, Louisa and your sister-in-law both got pregnant. How could it have been anything else but response, new life needed to revive some hope and joy in our family? And then in December, four days apart, two perfect girls were born, one fair and one dark, a balm for the wound that losing you had torn into their mothers. Your brother cried because you were not at the hospital—you were the first one there when his boys were born. Two girls to help us get through the first anniversaries, my mother's birthday and her death day, Christmas, and then January 3 and, a few weeks later, your birthday.

In early November your Uncle C died in surgery. Although he had been ill, the prognosis was positive, so we were very shocked. I visited him the day before; he was tied to a zillion machines, so many I could hardly get near his bed. It was very hard on your brother; you know he and Uncle C were close. Your poor father, Giana, his two younger brothers gone, and this one so soon after you. I was very angry with you when this happened. I couldn't help but feel that you should have been here to support your dad, not adding to his grief, and not once again shifting the burden to your siblings.

As Thanksgiving 2014 approached, I knew I could not sit around a table and look at a turkey, much less cook one. Memories of the year before, with you and my mother peaceful in the firelight, would not allow it. James, Jamie, and I went to New York and met Dina and her grandchildren. Everything we did was different from a typical Thanksgiving weekend, apart from taking the kids to the Macy's parade, stamping our feet in intermittent snow. We went out to dinner and no one had turkey. We went skating in Central Park, went to MOMA, to the 9/11 Memorial and Museum, now complete, and to the Museum of Natural History. We saw the Rockettes. We walked and walked, looked at Christmas windows, did a little shopping. I was distracted, which had been the objective.

And in November, M died. Louisa found out through Facebook. His mother called me in December while I was in Colorado, days after the baby was born. She was calling to tell me so that I might tell you—she was afraid that you would find out and, of course, be very upset. I had to tell her about you, that you had been gone for almost a year. She started crying. What was wrong with our children, she sobbed. M's death was something to do with a fire; I didn't really understand if it was connected to substance use. He had been in the hospital for a few months. If I'm grateful for anything, it's that you didn't have to know this.

For the first time in decades I did not buy a Christmas tree, I did not decorate, I did not send cards, I did not bake cookies, I did not host Christmas morning brunch with everyone in their pajamas, I did not cook Christmas dinner with my mother. I went to Colorado to see my new granddaughter. Every year since you've been gone, I dread my formerly favorite months: November, December, and January.

~

Ten days after Giana died, I went back to work. It was not a difficult decision. Louisa and her husband returned to Colorado, and everybody else went back to work. Of course. Life goes on, one of the most maddening clichés that the newly bereaved have to hear. Instead what we are thinking is *Stop all the clocks, cut off the telephone*.

Staying home and losing my mind was not an option.

I called a couple of my very best friends at work and asked them to tell everybody that I wanted people to talk to me only about work. I could not have dozens of people hugging me and asking me how I was doing and telling me how sorry they were —I knew I wouldn't be able to hold it together if people reacted that way. I told my friends that I would talk to people one-on-one when I was ready. To my amazement, it worked. People smiled and maybe said, "Good to have you back," or squeezed my shoulder. But for a long while, no one dropped into the seat across from my desk and talked about anything other than work. It was what I needed, to immerse myself as much as possible in planning, deadlines, outcomes. Occasionally I would be so absorbed that time would pass, maybe thirty minutes, when I would actually not think about Giana. Then when my mind turned to her, it was as if ice water had been thrown on me. I had a physical reaction, a rush of adrenaline, a swift intake of breath as the idea that she was gone, permanently gone, suddenly returned.

But I continued to have the odd moments of doubt about her actually being gone.

My siblings tried to convince me that I didn't need to help clean out my mother's apartment. On the contrary, I needed to very much. I needed to fill every minute with tasks. We discovered an enormous number of unknown things. More than once I said, "What was wrong with her that she didn't tell us about these things?" The apartment was like a clown car: how did she stuff so much into those closets and drawers? It was a panacea for my grief. Here were a dozen pearl necklaces: chokers, short strand, long strand, emerald clasp, two strand, diamond clasp. Some were broken. Suddenly it was urgent to find a jeweler who specialized in pearls who could identify how old they were (my mother's? grandmother's? great-grandmother's?); someone who could restring them and clean them and advise me on how to store them. And here were a dozen cameos of different sizes, in gold, in silver, one black. Must find a different jeweler for those.

There were hundreds of photographs, many over a hundred years old, which had to be sorted and identified and put into protective albums. I had to consult with elder cousins and historical societies and alumni associations. I had to investigate digitizing all of them.

Lace. Lots of lace. Matching colors and cuffs in various patterns, in white and in black. Lace shawls, lace mantillas, lace table runners. Handmade or machine made? How old? Finding a lace expert to consult with is a very challenging business. Thank God.

By the second week, Celeste was shepherding me to grief groups. The first one we went to was at a local hospital. I remember liter bottles of soda. One woman had lost her son to cancer. Another had lost her son when he fell down the stairs eighteen years earlier and cracked his head on the corner of a piece of furniture. *Eighteen years? She's been telling this story for eighteen years?* Perhaps the first glimmer of what lay ahead.

We decided to try a group specifically geared to people who had lost a loved one through substance use. I believe we showed up there before two weeks had passed. These meetings start with going around the room and people saying their names and telling their stories. Like AA. People groaned with sympathy when they realized how recently Giana had died. I overlooked the comments about how Giana was with my mother now and the comments about her being at peace in a better place. For a while the group was comforting. I was especially tuned in to a few people whose loss was three or four years old. They didn't cry, and they were calm. Occasionally some young women who were in residential treatment would come to the group, each having lost a parent or a boyfriend or a sibling. Most of the time they were shockingly matter-of-fact. Yes, they had used with their brother before he died. Yes, their father had sold everything the family owned and plunged them into homelessness to feed his addiction. My son started coming to the group as well. He forged a particular connection with a woman who had lost her only child, a son, and was unable to work because of her intense grief. Out in Colorado, Louisa started a similar group with the help of a therapist specializing in substance use disorder. In time there was a person in my group who talked continually about seeing her daughter in the kitchen, about her reluctance to leave her kitchen because she didn't want to miss the chance of seeing her daughter. Another person talked about going to mediums. *Whatever works*, I thought, *but this is not for me*. I joined an online group to which I remain connected.

~

On February 24, 2014, seven weeks after Giana's death, I wrote an email to Doug Tieman, the CEO of Caron. I was all the things that one would be after losing a child—shocked, devastatingly sad, angry, guilty, and wishing for answers that might help me to make sense of what I will never be able to fully embrace. I said, "I don't write this letter to blame Caron. However, I do think that in addition to Giana's inability to use the tools she had been given and to reach out to others, mistakes were made." I proceeded to outline concerns with Giana's discharge, the aftercare planning process, and the one-size-fits-all quality of her treatment, which was apparent to me even without having her medical records. I asked that Mr. Tieman review these concerns with his staff in the hope that changes could be made that would lead to better outcomes for patients with opioid addiction. I asked him to contact me when that review had been done. Mr. Tieman replied the very next day, expressing his condolences and saying that he had asked a senior clinical staff member to look into my concerns and contact me. A few weeks later I did receive a call from the vice president of treatment services, who began his call by expressing his condolences and telling me that he couldn't discuss Giana's case specifically. Of course not—after several decades working in children and family services, I am well aware of the need for an organization to guard its liability. The ensuing conversation was exceedingly vague with no decisive comment on any of the points I had raised in my letter. After this call, I knew that any further contact with Caron would serve no purpose. They clearly felt the same because I never heard from them again except for one telephone call about four months later from someone inviting me to a Caron event—a fundraiser maybe—in Philadelphia. The message left indicated that the caller didn't know Giana had died.

During those first months following Giana's death, I walked through life like a very taut string. I knew I had to manage myself carefully or I would snap. I say *walk*, not another word like *float* or *drift*, because in fact my every step was very purposeful, designed to keep me standing. I went to work, I took care of the dog, I worked on organizing my mother's stuff. Sympathy cards piled up; sometimes I read them, mostly I did not. I was aware of when I could read one and when I could not. I watched tennis and began reading the *Outlander* series, very long books. Most people read them for the love story. I read them to become absorbed in their immense amount of detail about odd things like herbal medicine in the 1700s, how to make scotch, distant battles on distant moors. Distractions. I also read them because the central character is able to travel in time, hurtling herself backward and forward through portals usually found in standing stone circles. Some other characters have the ability to do it as well. That's what I wanted: an opportunity to travel backward and change the future.

Apart from going to work, doing errands, and walking the dog, I went out and socialized very little. I didn't want to see people, except a few close friends, usually no more than two at a time. I wanted to control the conversation, wanted it to be my choice whether I talked about Giana and about "how I was doing." I definitely did not want to walk into a group of people and encounter the variety of reactions that I had experienced in work meetings held with partners, out of the office. Some people looked the other way. Other people, trying to be kind, pricked my professional demeanor with their sympathies. A few times I had to excuse myself and go to the ladies room to take a few deep breaths and regain composure. Worst, people who didn't know would greet me as always, cheerfully, "Hey, Elise, what's up?" It was, of course, nobody's fault. There was no good way.

It was odd how formerly close friends responded. Some people did it with ease: *can I come over and have a cup of tea?* And then when there, quiet sympathy and an intuitive sense of what not to say. There were a lot of people I did not hear from. Certainly one reason is that people simply didn't know what to say, whether outreach would be welcome or not. I also realized later that I embodied a parent's worst nightmare—the problem you can't fix, the disease you can't cure, the phone call in the night. For some people, it was much easier just to ignore me.

I watched out for the emotional minefields in my house. When I had to go into the basement, I avoided looking into the corner where the bins containing Giana's stuff sat. I stopped using the Crock-Pot; in fact, I barely cooked at all. I closed the door to the guest room where she had primarily stayed so I wouldn't see ghosts of her through the open doorway. But occasionally I had a full-blown fantasy attack.

The doorbell rings and Jade jumps up and then goes to her toy basket, which is what she does when someone she knows is at the door. She greets them with a toy. I see you through the small windows at the top of the door, your expression both anxious and excited. I fumble getting the door open. Jade is all over you, jumping up and down, and I'm pushing her out of the way, trying to hug you.

We're both crying. You look almost the same, a bit too thin, your thick dark hair waving all the way to your waist.

"I had to be far away to get well," you say. "I didn't think they would say that I was dead. It's all a big mix-up."

I'm stunned, angry, confused, but all of that is overshadowed by the joy I feel. You're back!

The moment passes.

~

Shortly after Giana's death, my children came up with the idea of erecting a memorial bench in the park where we had her service, the park where we had all spent time with Giana and her dogs. I don't know if I was a part of the conversations leading to this decision: I have no recollection of it. I know that my daughters collected money from people who wanted to do something. I know that Celeste meticulously organized the cards that came with the money into a binder, each card in a sleeve. I recall meeting Lou and my son at the park to confer with a city worker about the placement of the bench, and that there were piles of snow and it was muddy. I did not contribute to the wording on the plaque that would go on the bench, although I'm sure the kids asked me if I approved. It says:

IN LOVING MEMORY OF
GIANA NATALI
DAUGHTER, SISTER, NIECE
AUNT, COUSIN, AND FRIEND
MAY YOU BE HAPPY AND FREE
1.21.80–1.3.14

The rest is a blur, until one of my kids said that the bench had been installed, and then the planning for a dedication ceremony began. There was a lot of back and forth about dates, and I remember uncharacteristically losing my temper and saying something like, *I don't care about the bench! I don't want a bench! I want my child!* My patience was not what it had been, and that remains true.

But finally we did have a gathering in the park by the bench. It was summer, about six months after Giana died. The misty park, the snowy park, had been transformed into the deep, heavy green that follows a wet winter and spring in Philadelphia. We had food delivered, and we brought pictures and relics and put them on folding tables. As we set up, my nephews and grandsons were playing soccer in the park. Louisa, who had flown in, stood talking with my daughter-in-law, comparing pregnancy notes.

Life goes on. Stop the clocks. . . .

There were a lot of people there, but mostly they were friends of mine and Lou's, friends of my older children, not friends of Giana's. Several teachers from her school came, the K–12 school where she spent thirteen years and was, I think, at her happiest. Giana had isolated herself so completely that when she died, she had few friends. Several teammates from her swim team came, and one old friend from high school. It had been so long since I had seen her that at first I didn't recognize her. She told me she had three children, which tore me apart, thinking about what might have been for Giana. I was very grateful to them for coming. It helped me to feel that however Giana had fractured her relationships in more recent years, some people reached back and remembered her as she once was. She was so much more than the mental illness and addiction of the last years of her life.

Celeste, sometimes stopping to gather herself, did most of the talking at the short program as we dedicated the bench. I can't remember if anyone else spoke. I sat near the front for a while on a blanket with the grandchildren and then got up and stood beside Louisa, who was crying. A friend of Lou's played his guitar and sang "Amazing Grace," a hymn I never want to hear again.

People donated so much money that we had six times what the bench cost. My kids decided to donate the money to a rescue shelter where a playroom for dogs was dedicated to Giana. I have been there and, of course, to the bench in the intervening years. For some people in the family, the bench is a source of comfort. But not for me. When I go there, I see Giana chasing Abby around the pond until Abby goes flying into the water. I see Giana patiently walking with Maggie, her three-legged rescue boxer. I see Giana standing in a knot of other dog owners, chatting, as the dogs run in circles. I cannot recall those scenes and feel any sense of comfort, only a searing ache for her. Maybe that will change.

Chapter Eighteen

The veterans of loss say that time moves one to acceptance. So this is how it happens.

One Christmas—seven years ago?—three years before you died?—time is only before and after—you wanted a jacket for Christmas. You were very specific. North Face. A certain length and pocket placement, detachable hood. I searched and found the right one at REI. You loved it and wore it all the time.

You asked me to bring it to Caron, so I had it dry-cleaned and brought it to you. When I visited you at Caron as the weather got colder, I would come over the hill from the parking lot and see you down by the gazebo, your typical question mark posture endearing, wearing the jacket, sometimes with hood up if it was really cold.

When you died, your brother-in-law went to The Rose House and brought back your stuff. The next few times I went to their house after you died—for Louisa's shower, where my throat hurt from holding back tears, and a few months later when your niece was born—I knew your stuff was somewhere in the house. I would glide by closets that I had no reason to go in, and wonder, but I didn't look. We were fragile, and then we had the brand new baby. Like every new, first-time mother, your sister was sleep deprived, nervous, hormonal. She didn't need me to be mourning over your relics.

The next time I visited, when the baby was three months old, I found all your stuff in a closet in the basement. I was compelled to look for it one day when I was alone. I opened a box, and there was the jacket. I pushed my face into the lining and smelled you, the fur around the hood smelled like your hair products. I pulled gloves from the pockets that smelled like cigarette smoke and realized that you probably had worn the jacket that terrible day. I howled. I wrapped myself in the jacket and sobbed.

In a side pocket I found a commemorative coin from Caron engraved with the ubiquitous serenity prayer: *God grant me the serenity to accept the things I cannot change; courage to change the things I can; and wisdom to know the difference.* It felt like a cruel joke.

I brought the jacket up to my guest room and put it in my suitcase to bring home. At home, I hung it in my closet, the last in a line of jackets and coats. Sometimes I would slip out my chosen coat and avoid looking at yours; other days I would bring it out and cry into it. After a while I would squeeze it each time I went into that closet. Then after that, sometimes I didn't touch it but just looked at it on the hanger in the back, acknowledging it as part of the solid, stationary lump of grief that I carry with me. Sometimes when I see it, I tell you to come and get it.

It hasn't happened yet that I go into that closet and forget the jacket is there.

~

Buried in Celeste's house were the relics that Louisa had brought with her when she and her husband came home the week after Giana died, except for the ashes, which somehow ended up in my brother's house. In Colorado, Giana and her stuff had been scattered in several places. My son-in-law picked up what was in the house where she died—some clothes, jewelry, books, CDs, journals, toiletries, documents (when do personal papers become documents?)—and packed them away in a closet in their house. The funeral home had her ashes and her hair, which Louisa brought to Philly.

Even though I was at Celeste's house at least weekly, it was several months before I finally told her I wanted to see Giana's hair. She wavered, worried about me and also apprehensive herself. She had not looked at it either. She brought it into the bathroom, and we shut the door, not wanting the kids to interrupt us. Some caring person at the funeral home had put it into a rectangular white box, about the size of a gift box for a scarf. It was coiled in tissue paper and tied at two-inch intervals with yarn. When we opened the box, the smell of freshly shampooed hair was strong. I thought about how on the morning of the day she died, Giana had gotten up as if it was any other day and washed her hair.

~

Perhaps the funeral home had the clothes and jewelry that she was wearing when she died, or maybe the coroner's office had those. I don't know what clothes she was wearing or what happened to them. Celeste has the necklace Giana was wearing. Louisa wears the ring that Giana was wearing, a ring that Louisa had designed and given to her, but I don't know if she got it from the coroner or the funeral home. Who takes off the jewelry? Maybe the coroner had her handbag, or maybe the police had it and then gave it to the funeral home. Someone official had itemized everything in it, and someone gave the package to Louisa, and she brought it home and gave it to Celeste. I finally looked at it when Celeste was packing up her house to move. She asked if I wanted her to take it with her or whether I wanted to take it. Almost three years had passed.

Contents of one brown faux leather purse:

A brown wallet containing receipts, Pennsylvania driver's license, insurance cards, three bus tickets, $3 in bills, $2.84 in change.

One tube pink lip gloss

One tube Blistex

Three bobby pins

Two pens

One key

Brochure of Boulder County AA meetings

Two tampons

One cigarette pack containing two cigarettes

Documentation of a life.

The police kept her phone for a long time while they tried to find the source of the text that was clearly from the person who sold her the heroin that killed her. His name was Mike.

~

In 2015 publicity about the opioid epidemic exploded. Newspaper articles about overdoses led me to articles about treatment and opioid prescribing that led me to studies that led me to government agencies that led me to more research. Some of the misgivings I had felt during Giana's illness and treatment resurfaced as I learned more, as did my guilt for not delving into this assiduously while Giana was living.

I wanted to read her medical records against this new backdrop of information. In a family full of lawyers, I knew we could access Giana's medical records simply by establishing her estate and requesting them. On a stormy October day in 2015, Lou and I met at City Hall to open the estate. The process itself was very simple; the emotions were not. Opening the estate was yet another acknowledgment that she was really gone. I cried in front of strangers while signing the documents. I suppose those workers are accustomed to this.

The court gives you certified forms to send with your requests. We sent them to every provider we knew who had seen Giana. Some requested that we pay for the records, which we did; some sent them quickly and without any communication. As they were received, I skimmed through them. I was busy working on my novel, *Watermark*, which had been put aside when Giana died. And I wasn't quite ready to read them thoroughly.

At the end of August 2015, twenty months after Giana's death, I left my job. I was about to turn sixty-four. While I was very committed to the mission of our work, there were changes that made staying difficult—a new CEO who, I suspected, would make massive changes that I would disagree with, and a board that I felt was barely competent, only marginally committed to the agency, with little understanding of how the organization's work was actually accomplished. I wasn't sure what I was going to do, but I wasn't apprehensive: how could I be fearful about leaving a job after losing Giana? The worst thing that could ever happen to me had already happened. Freed from the daily beat of work demands, the novel flowed easily, but I still created many distracting tasks for the time that I wasn't writing. I read every night for many hours. I spent every Saturday at the art museum. I took out memberships at the zoo, the children's museum, the museum of natural history, an arboretum. I took the grandchildren everywhere.

Meanwhile, we received nothing from The Rose House. Our first written request to them had been sent on October 20, 2015. On December 21, 2015, I sent a follow-up letter, referencing the first request. Still nothing. After the holidays I started calling. The primary number was never answered, and I received no return call to my messages. Finally I decided to start hitting every extension in turn until someone answered, and eventually someone did. It was a man who identified himself by name and said he was an administrator. When I explained the situation, he stated that he wasn't going to send me any records just on the basis of a letter. I reiterated that my original letter had been accompanied by a court order and that he didn't have a choice about sending them. He said he would look into it and get back to me. He never did. When I called again and finally tracked him down, he told me that they couldn't find any records.

That was the last straw, so I contacted a person at the State of Colorado office that licenses substance use treatment programs. When I explained that I was trying to get the medical-records for my daughter who had died while a resident at The Rose House, the worker inhaled deeply, paused, and then asked me to repeat what I had said. When I did, she told me in an alarmed voice that she had no information about someone dying at The Rose House. In a few minutes we cleared up the confusion: at the time Giana was a resident there, the facility had been unlicensed. Now it was my turn to be dumbfounded—the facility was unlicensed? How could that be? The efficient and sympathetic person with whom I spoke explained that in Colorado, such programs are only required to be licensed if a referring agency, such as the court, requires it, or if they are receiving public funding. I asked about food prep and related regulation; surely there were health regulations in place to inspect facilities that feed a certain number of people. The worker explained that a lot of programs get around this by having patients shop for and prepare their own food, as Giana had done. I tried to imagine this at the main Rose House facility, where sixteen women resided. I asked about oversight of dispensing medication, and she replied that they get around this by having the medication prescribed by a contracted physician, and therefore they are not officially dispensing it.

Finally I asked about staff qualifications, as the CEO/founder of The Rose House was not currently licensed according to the state database. The state employee replied that it was not necessary for her to be licensed if she was not herself providing treatment. I was stunned. Of course I looked up all these regulations, and the worker was correct on every one. Like some other facilities, The Rose House did not move to get licensed until the Affordable Care Act (ACA) was in full force and more treatment dollars started flowing, which was after Giana's death.

This means that at the time of Giana's stay at The Rose House, there was no oversight at all of the content of "treatment" or the performance of staff, except that provided by a person who was herself not currently credentialed.

Every state has different regulations for substance use treatment facilities and the staff who work in them, and there are wide differences. Because substance use treatment has never been considered part of the medical treatment system, the regulatory bar and staffing standards are generally much lower. This has begun to change, albeit slowly, with the passage of the Paul Wellstone and Peter Domenici Mental Health Parity and Addiction Equity Act and the ACA. The problem has been widely recognized; in the 2012 CASA report, it is noted that "government and professional oversight of addiction treatment facilities and programs is insufficient to insure that patients receive clinically-indicated, quality care" (187). Of course, there can't be any oversight whatsoever if a program like The Rose House is operating wholly unlicensed. I assume there are still rehab facilities in Colorado that don't receive government funding or accept patients from referral sources that require licensing and thus are still able to operate without any oversight.

I don't know whether the state worker contacted The Rose House on my behalf to get the ball rolling on the records release, or whether The Rose House got tired of my calls and emails. In any event, in mid-March I finally received a reply from the CEO of The Rose House, which stated: "We recently switched from hard copy records to electronic medical records.

It is my understanding that Giana's records haven't been located."

More emails, more phone calls to the helpful state worker. We eventually received the records at the end of March 2016. I had asked for the psychiatrist's records, but The Rose House stated that because the psychiatrist was a contractor, they didn't have his records. I had already sent him a separate request. The post office was unable to secure a signature for the request that we sent him, and it was returned to us. Phone calls to the psychiatrist were not returned.

My novel was published in April of 2016. For a few months afterward, I was busy with book readings, book clubs, interviews, and publicity work. As that slowed, I started a careful chronological reading of the records. From the records, I learned some details that I didn't know about. The coroner's office listed her time of death as 10:25 p.m. I know that isn't correct, because in a "Critical Event Report" written by her Rose House therapist, he states that Giana's roommates called him "hysterical" at about 10:00 p.m., and she was dead when they called. Her roommates found her "slumped" facedown on her bed and when they tried to rouse her, discovered she was not breathing and her body was cold. He describes some phone calls between administrators about who should go to the house.

All I could think about was that if the roommates had come home an hour earlier, she would not have died that night.

How does a person die from a heroin overdose? Many people have observed a similar process when a dying loved one, often already unconscious, is given increasingly large doses of morphine. Basically, breathing is depressed, and eventually the person stops breathing. I have been told that it is like falling into a deep, peaceful sleep: no struggle, no panic. I must believe that. I believe that she used that evening, and having been abstinent for almost six months, she used more than she could handle, a very common story of overdose. I do believe she was so depressed that she felt hopeless, and she had little will to remain abstinent.

After my first full reading of the records, I began again, this time correlating parts of the notes with what I was learning from reading research reports and studies. I began writing small sections, some personal vignettes, others based on the notes and the research. I wasn't sure where this was going, especially in terms of form, but by Christmas of 2016, I was writing in earnest.

~

This year and a half of writing and research has been searing, infuriating, empowering. As usual, I have been speaking my mind. I served on the Philadelphia Mayor's Opioid Task Force, where I was inspired by most of the people I met, especially the medical professionals—smart, well-informed, hardworking people who bring their medical understanding to policy. As a result of that experience, I was asked to serve on the advisory board of the Department of Behavioral Health, an honor. More great people, including treatment providers!

I have gone to public forums and city council hearings to tell our story, Giana, yours and mine, and have discovered, sadly, that there is still a lot of stigma and misinformation.

To do all this, I rewrote the serenity prayer: *Take a deep breath and find the courage and wisdom to change the things you cannot accept.*

And now the book is nearing an end. Now I am worrying about agents, publishers, promotion. *Life goes on, stop the clocks . . .*

Chapter Nineteen

February 20, 2018: Your ashes are sitting on a dresser in my bedroom, a dresser I took from my mother's and which, before that, was in my grandmother's bedroom for as long as I can remember. Well, most of your ashes are sitting there. I still have some of them in the small personal urn we were each given four years ago, and maybe your dad and your sisters do also. Not your brother, though. I believe he scattered the last of his at the beach, into the waves. Isn't it a really odd idea that you are in a number of places at once?

Your ashes were at my brother's house for three years. Several times when I was there, I almost asked for them, but the anticipation about how I would feel was too upsetting. Finally, though, I let him know before a visit that I wanted them. When we left, he handed them to James, and when we got to my house, James carried them in and put them on the dresser. They are in a rectangular stone urn, a deep maroon color like the purplish underbelly of a pending thunderstorm, with white swirls like wind-driven clouds floating near the surface. I have no idea where that urn came from. The ashes sit in that urn, and honestly I feel little relationship to them. I have a hard time relating what I know is in that urn to the tall strong body, the chiseled face, the dimple on the chin, the wide smile, the thick curly eyelashes, the slender ankles and graceful fingers that were you.

When I die, I am going to have my ashes and your ashes put into biodegradable urns, ones that will disintegrate, and have them buried together. Then as the urns dissolve, we will begin to move through the soil and eventually into plants whose seeds will scatter. Ashes to ashes and dust to dust.

The Great Ones say it in strikingly similar ways.

"The amazing thing is that every atom in your body came from a star that exploded. And the atoms in your left hand probably came from a different star than your right hand. It really is the most poetic thing I know about physics: You are all stardust. . . The stars died so that you could be here today." Lawrence M. Krauss, *A Universe from Nothing: Why There Is Something Rather Than Nothing*

"We are stardust. In the highest exalted way one can use that phrase." Neil DeGrasse Tyson, 2013

"Whether we're born in San Francisco, or Sudan, or close to the heart of the Milky Way galaxy, we are the products of a billion-year lineage of wandering stardust." So said Jill Tarter in her 2009 TED talk, "Join the SETI Search."

That's it. We will be stardust, wandering together.

~

Recently I have started wearing your stuff. Using your stuff. It started when I was at Louisa's over the holidays, and I went back to the closet that I had begun to unpack a few years earlier, when I took your jacket. I hadn't been back in there since, but they are about to remodel their basement, so we had to figure out what to do with your stuff. So ordinary, isn't it? They are about to remodel their basement. It's just that with every change, large and small, the world is not recognizable as the one you left. That also seems like a commonplace thought, yet I seem to have difficulty fully accepting it. Some days I mentally list what has changed and what remains the same. The before and after.

The last time I had been in that closet, I just took out the jacket and papers, journals and documents, but didn't look through your clothes, shoes, cosmetics, and other stuff. This time I looked through everything. Louisa came downstairs from time to time, scurrying back upstairs when certain familiar items came out of the boxes and bins. I told her that we needed to throw out your cosmetics and toiletries—half-full bottles of shampoo and conditioner, used deodorant. She told me she didn't want to know about it, so I discreetly put it all in a plastic bag and dropped it into the outdoor trash bin. I brought home a full bottle of scented body lotion that I have been using from time to time.

I found the Christmas socks I had given you in your Christmas stocking, only a week before you died. For some reason you had worn the anklets but not the others. It looked as if the anklets might have been thrown into the box straight from a hamper; they didn't look washed. As I tend to do with all of your stuff, I smelled them. If they were unwashed, the intervening years had erased their scent. There were two other pairs, both featuring Christmas dogs, still in their packaging. I brought these socks home and have been wearing them since. In my dresser they're mixed in with my own socks, but I know which are yours.

I also brought home the pair of rain boots we'd bought one Sunday with Dad when you were at Caron. We bought them because you were going on a camping trip, a sober recreational adventure described as a way to demonstrate to you and the other patients that you can have fun activities without drugs or alcohol. They are mid-calf height, sturdy, with a tartan pattern of pale green, gray, and pink. I am certain that you never wore them. They were immaculate, too clean to have been worn in mud or even in the woods. I have been wearing them through these past muddy, rainy, slushy weeks.

And then just a few days ago, I went back into the bin in my basement to look at the list that came home with your purse. I emptied your wallet, a wallet I gave you, a wallet that you loved, and carefully put all of the cards and receipts into plastic wrapping and put them back into your purse. And then I emptied my wallet into yours.

From the very first week you were gone, Celeste wanted to wear your clothes. It's taken me four years to get some comfort from these reminders of you.

~

I went to an exhibit at the Barnes featuring works by Anselm Kiefer and Rodin. The exhibit was occasioned by the republication of Rodin's book on French cathedrals, a mix of drawings and watercolors and text; the exhibit's premise is Kiefer's response to these. Apparently Rodin felt that the cathedrals should not be restored and repaired if they were not in use—they belonged to their historical and cultural time and should be allowed to disintegrate. The show is very complex, but a part of Kiefer's work here is a riff on impermanence. Here's how this relates to you. In a large vitrine titled *Die Walkuren* (*The Valkyries*, yes, the Norse mythical creatures and Wagner, the title being another subject altogether, although perhaps relevant because in the mythology, the Valkyries get to decide who lives and who dies in battle), Kiefer displays articles of clothing—a child's nightgown, an infant dress, a bra, pants, and so on—perhaps fifteen articles in all, hanging from a rod. On the bottom of the vitrine is a surface that looks like earth after a drought, cracked and gray, with a large pile of rocky objects sitting on the creviced surface—an uninviting landscape. The pieces of clothing have been coated with plaster so they are stiff, so they don't hang as typical clothing would but are animated, almost as if they have adopted the pose of the last wearer. In places the plaster is breaking and flaking, so the fabric is showing. The plaster has been painted or decorated with acrylic, clay, lead—who knows what?—with original embellishments like tiny pearl buttons gleaming through the plaster, haunting and beautiful. I walked around this vitrine and looked at the pieces of clothing from all sides, and suddenly my eyes were welling. It was like a comment on what I have been doing with so much of your stuff—arranging your kindergarten drawings into scrapbooks, putting your baby clothes in shadow boxes, organizing your photos into albums—trying in vain to preserve pieces in order to defy change, to prevent the inevitable decomposition of the objects that represent you.

In one of your journal entries, you say, "I've been having good insights and talking about good issues, but I can't feel anything. I just intellectualize it all." You can't feel anything because you intellectualize as one strategy—like starving yourself, self-medicating with drugs—to avoid feeling anything. Intellectualize everything . . . wonder where you got that from?

~

That first anniversary of Giana's death, I made the terrible mistake of coming back from my Colorado Christmas before January 3. I spent the morning at the vet with Jade. Jade had a horrible rash, and I felt I needed to take her. How ironic, that I was at the vet where Giana used to work, with the dog that shouldn't be mine. My plan had been to meet Lou and the kids at the bench and then go out to lunch with them. By the time I left the vet, it was sleeting, and I certainly didn't want food. I just took Jade home and cuddled up with her under a throw blanket on the sofa, the way Giana used to. Every January 3 since then, I have made sure to be in Colorado, and Louisa and I have planned something to do—take the little one to the aquarium, to the children's museum, to the ski slopes.

~

So now, four years out, how is it? That old adage, that time heals all wounds, isn't true. I think time often does heal the wound of the jilted lover, and perhaps the sorrow of losing an aged parent. Now when I think about my mother, it is usually with a smile, albeit accompanied by a pang. But I suspect that for most people, time does not heal the loss of a child. I have a cousin who lost a child over forty years ago at the age of two. She still tears up sometimes when talking about her. Right now, for me, I am carrying Giana with me as I move haltingly forward. I think I'm more fortunate than some. I have other children and grandchildren who give me joy; I have many others in my life: siblings, nieces and nephews, cousins old and young, friends. I have always found fulfillment and relief in work. I have many interests that are not just distracting but satisfying. And for some reason that I cannot explain except through the accident of genetics, I have the resilience gene that Giana did not inherit. Sadly, I have spoken to many other grieving parents who are disabled by their grief, unable to find any way forward. One thing is certain; it's different for everyone.

I wonder how it is for JM's mother, the bodybuilder, the introduction to Nubain and the pathway to heroin and death. He died himself, a needle in his arm, a few months ago. I feel very badly for his parents; for him I feel nothing.

I see how it is for my other children, my daughters' brittle anxieties about their children ever apparent, and for my son, guilt and sadness always close to the surface.

I find that it's not only Giana's absence that aches; it's her presence. She was a few weeks short of thirty-four when she died, and there is a reminder of her at every turn. Although she did not grow up in the house I live in now, she spent long periods of fifteen years here. Her ghost is in every room. If I'm in Philadelphia, it's an unusual car ride that doesn't take me past a place that holds a memory of her. On the very day that I am writing this, I had to tell someone I ran into, an acquaintance from long ago, that she had died. It happens less frequently, but it still happens, when people ask the chatty question, "So what are your kids up to?" So one would think that fleeing to a place where there are no memories of her would be a relief, and often it is, for a while. And then I suddenly find that I am virulently homesick because I want to be as near to her as I can be.

Carrying her with me. She is always with me, which is both what I want and what causes sorrow. It's a dichotomy that won't be resolved. Certainly part of the reason I wrote this book was to keep my connection to her not just present but changing—I am encountering her in new circumstances every time I read a medical note, look at worksheets written in her hand, read entries from her journal. She has grown for me even though she has died. I have only recently begun to explore and empty the storage unit that contains the bulk of her furniture, clothing, books, and so forth that was stored in the spring of 2013. I've been paying for that unit every month since but have been unable to enter it until now.

I know there will come a point where everything that I can know about her will be known. I dread that time.

~

In one of your journals you ask: Who am I if I am not a swimmer?

In another you ask: Who am I if I cannot practice my profession?

And for four years I have been asking: Who am I if I am not your mother?

To answer your questions, neither your activity nor your illness defined you: you are a most beloved daughter, granddaughter, sister, aunt, niece, cousin, and friend to people and animals. You are kind, sensitive, bright, shy, Italian, witty, vulnerable, affectionate, curious, fragile, organized, self-critical, introspective, hardworking, quiet, needy, loving.

And the answer to my own question, understood all the more pointedly after the sorrow and complexity of the past four years, is that I will always be your mother.

Giana's bench the day it was installed:

July 26, 2014

Afterword

September 2018: So the work on this book is coming to a close, as it must. In the course of writing it, I have discovered things about Giana that I didn't know, and I was able to maintain closeness to her in an odd but comforting way. People have asked me if writing it has been cathartic. If that means I have "purged" my strong feelings, then no. All of my feelings related to her—love, sorrow, pride, regret, anger, admiration—that soup of boiling emotions—remain intact. But if not catharsis, at least satisfaction. I have told truths about her and her story that I needed to tell, and there will be more to say, in other ways, because she is always with me.

I do need to say that I understand very well how fortunate we were in some respects: Giana didn't live in a tent in a heroin encampment beside railroad tracks; she received speedy treatment (although not effective treatment) because she had insurance and the skills to advocate for herself and, when that didn't work, a supportive family who could raise resources and advocate for her; she had no related health problems like abscesses and heart valve issues; she didn't spend time in jail. In addition to the fact that she actually only used heroin for fifteen months and half of that time she was sober, this is certainly related to class and race and the role it plays in America, and that is why, at least initially, the attention paid to the opioid crisis was criticized in contrast to the draconian policies that characterized the response to the crack epidemic that ravaged communities of color in the eighties and nineties. Critics claimed that attention was only being paid because the victims were white. While acknowledging the obvious social justice issues, I don't think this binary analysis is helpful or necessary: are our expectations so low that we can't advocate for solutions to the current crisis as well as demand criminal justice reform and reparative investments in our communities of color at the same time?

But in fact, whatever her privilege may have been, Giana died. Ironically, this supports one of the clichés about heroin—its's an equal opportunity killer. In the past eighteen months, use of opioids by Hispanics and African Americans has increased. This is supported by data, including a large jump in hospital admissions of those populations for heroin and fentanyl overdose.

By trying to understand what happened to Giana, I have formed strong opinions about the best ways to approach the opioid epidemic from a policy perspective. First and foremost, the federal government must stop floundering and provide real leadership and funding in collaboration with states and local governments. Canada and most European countries are doing a much better job than we are; there is no need to re-create the wheel. Strategies that work are in place elsewhere, and we need to adopt them.

We must decriminalize use of all drugs at all levels of government and redirect those criminal justice resources to prevention and treatment. Incarcerating nonviolent users rather than directing them immediately into treatment is wasteful and ineffective. Treatment rather than imprisonment is happening in some places through drug courts, but this should be a coordinated national strategy, and decriminalization is needed to move forward with other interventions like safe injection sites.

I am not suggesting legalization of heroin, fentanyl, and so forth, the way marijuana is being legalized for recreational use. Law enforcement should continue to prosecute large trafficking and distribution networks. Law enforcement should also continue to prosecute pharmaceutical companies that prioritize profit over population health.

We should continue to adopt common sense prescribing policies for opioids while assuring that patients experiencing pain from major surgeries, cancer, and other very serious conditions receive relief. Other approaches to chronic but not severe pain must be developed and implemented even if they are more expensive than pills. While states are doing this, a national database for prescribers should be developed to flag both pill-shoppers and overprescribing medical professionals. In many locations it's a quick trip to another state, so information sharing between states is vital.

The foundation of every policy approach must be harm reduction. We need to keep people alive so they can get well. This means on-demand access to high-quality and evidence-based treatment regardless of the insurance payer. Here we have once again the coverage issues related to health care in the United States, where access to Medicaid varies by state, some people are still uninsured, and who and what will be covered is a political football that is always in the air. (To understand the difficulties of accessing treatment and the lack of coordination among systems, as well as a good discussion about bias against MAT and its consequences, I recommend reading Beth Macy's recent book *Dopesick*.)

We need national standards that delineate who can treat people with addiction and what that treatment should be. Our best shot to achieve this is to bring the treatment and recovery systems wholly into our health care systems so they are properly licensed, regulated, and overseen. In the short run this will be very expensive; in the long run it will save lives and money.

We need to refine our approach to prevention. Universal prevention campaigns in schools, while not eliminated, should be curtailed in favor of prevention strategies aimed at high-risk populations. We know a lot about this now and need to use our knowledge to direct our prevention resources and efforts. Universal campaigns to educate the general public and reduce stigma are important, both as a prevention measure and also to enhance advocacy for proven interventions.

These are only broad policy ideas. Becoming involved with advocacy is a segue to more information and more local concerns, as well as a palliative to the frustration opioid use disorder creates. One of the reasons I wrote this book was to share my experience with other families dealing with OUD and provide a context to think about what is happening to a loved one and what to do. Here are a few summarized ideas:

- Act immediately and aggressively if you suspect your loved one is in danger—early intervention improves outcomes.
- Seek medical intervention by qualified addiction medicine doctors, and carefully check the professional credentials of staff. Therapists should be professionally qualified as therapists, for example.
- Shame and stigma will only hurt your efforts to help. Addiction is a chronic, relapsing disease, and allowing people, especially treatment staff, to blame the patient should never be tolerated. Reject anything that implies "character defects."
- Research into opioids continues at a quick pace, and thus the best practices of treatment will change as well. Make sure you do your homework, and if something doesn't seem to be working, insist that changes are made. At this writing, although there is still plenty of unnecessary controversy, there is no argument about the effectiveness of medication-assisted treatment; it will increase the chances that your loved one will cease using and that the OUD will remain in remission.

- Understand from the beginning that OUD is a lifelong medical issue. Your loved one's disease may go into remission, but vigilance will be necessary for life. This may require very hard decisions. For example, I realize now that if Giana had survived, she would never again have been able to work in a vet hospital with access to opioids and benzodiazepines.
- This disease is characterized by relapse. Given its lethality, efforts to prevent relapse are critical. Act immediately if you suspect that a person in recovery is relapsing.
- Do not allow your loved one's opioid use disorder needs to be treated entirely in integration with other substance use disorders. "One size fits all" does not work.
- Most people with OUD have co-occurring mental health disorders. These must be treated as well and as aggressively as the OUD.
- Ignore phrases like "tough love," "codependency," and "they need to hit bottom." It is desirable for you to insist that your loved one comply with treatment recommendations and for you to put in place strategies to make that more likely. Be outspoken and insistent, but do it with compassion and love.

Yes, do it with love.

Sources and Resources

U.S. Department of Health and Human Services (HHS), Office of the Surgeon General. November 2016. *Facing Addiction in America: The Surgeon General's Report on Alcohol, Drugs, and Health.* Washington, DC: HHS.

Center on Addiction. June 2012. *Addiction Medicine: Closing the Gap between Science and Practice.* www.centeronaddiction.org/addiction-research/reports/addiction-medicine-closing-gap-between-science-and-practice

Fletcher, Anne M. 2013. *Inside Rehab: The Surprising Truth About Addiction Treatment—and How to Get Help That Works.* New York: Penguin Books.

Macy, Beth. 2018. *Dopesick: Dealers, Doctors, and the Drug Company that Addicted America.* New York: Little, Brown and Company.

Quinones, Sam. 2015. *Dreamland: The True Tale of America's Opiate Addiction.* New York: Bloomsbury Press.

Websites

American Society of Addiction Medicine

www.asam.org

National Institute on Drug Abuse

www.nida.nih.gov

Substance Abuse and Mental Health Services Administration

www.samhsa.gov

Acknowledgments

I couldn't have written this memoir without the support of my family, especially and including Giana's father, Louis Natali. I greatly appreciate their advice, support, reads, and rereads.

I am indebted to my very close friend, Dina Portnoy, for her compassion, and for her reflections on the manuscript at various stages.

I am very grateful to my therapist, Emma Steiner, for helping me to recover my equilibrium and her keen insights about addiction.

I have been a member of a writing group called the FISH for over twenty years. As usual, their constructive criticism made this a better book.

Finally, many thanks to my friends and colleagues in the advocacy and recovery community for their support and encouragement.

ABOUT THE AUTHOR

Photo credit: Jermaine Parker

Elise Schiller has been writing fiction and actively participating in writing groups since adolescence. After a thirty-year career in education and family services in Philadelphia, she retired to write full time. She is currently working on a fiction series about Philadelphia; SparkPress will be publishing the first book in the series. Schiller sits on the advisory board of the Philadelphia Department of Behavioral Health and Intellectual disAbility Services (DBHIDS), and she has served on the Philadelphia Mayor's Task Force on the Opioid Epidemic. When not writing, reading, or volunteering, she enjoys visiting museums and historical sites, often with one of her seven grandchildren or various nieces and nephews in tow.

SELECTED TITLES FROM SPARKPRESS

SparkPress is an independent boutique publisher delivering high-quality, entertaining, and engaging content that enhances readers' lives, with a special focus on female-driven work. www.gosparkpress.com.

Love You Like the Sky: Surviving the Suicide of a Beloved, Sarah Neustadter. $16.95, 978-1-943006-88-5. Part memoir and part self-help in nature, this compilation of emails—written by a young psychologist to her beloved following his suicide—chronicles the process of surviving and grieving the tragic death of a loved one, and of using grief for deeper psychospiritual healing and transformation.

The House that Made Me: Writers Reflect on the Places and People That Defined Them, edited by Grant Jarrett. $17, 978-1-940716-31-2. In this candid, evocative collection of essays, a diverse group of acclaimed authors reflect on the diverse homes, neighborhoods, and experiences that helped shape them—using Google Earth software to revisit the location in the process.

A Story That Matters: A Gratifying Approach to Writing About Your Life, Gina Carroll. $16.95, 9-781-943006-12-0. With each chapter focusing on stories from the seminal periods of a lifetime—motherhood, childhood, relationships, work, and spirit—*A Story That Matters* provides the tools and motivation to craft and complete the stories of your life.

The Rules of Half: A Novel, Jenna Patrick. $16.95, 978-1-943006-18-2. When an orphaned teen claims he's her biological father, Will Fletcher—a manic-depressant who's sworn to never be a parent again—must come to terms with his illness and his tragic past if he is to save her from the streets. This explores what it is to be an atypical family in a small town and to be mentally ill in the wake of a tragedy.

The Half-Life of Remorse: A Novel, Grant Jarrett. $16.95, 978-1-943006-14-4. Three life-scarred people are brought together to confront each other thirty years after the brutal crime that shattered their lives, and as the puzzle of the past gradually falls together, the truth commands a high price.

ABOUT SPARKPRESS

SparkPress is an independent, hybrid imprint focused on merging the best of the traditional publishing model with new and innovative strategies. We deliver high-quality, entertaining, and engaging content that enhances readers' lives. We are proud to bring to market a list of *New York Times* best-selling, award-winning, and debut authors who represent a wide array of genres, as well as our established, industry-wide reputation for creative, results-driven success in working with authors. SparkPress, a BookSparks imprint, is a division of SparkPoint Studio LLC.

Learn more at GoSparkPress.com